ROOF EXPLORER'S GUIDE
101 NEW YORK CITY ROOFTOPS

BY LESLIE ADATTO

LESLIE ADATTO
NEW YORK, NEW YORK 10014

Text ©2014 by Leslie Adatto
Photographs: Heather Shimmin and Ari Burling
Book Design: Arlene Bender, Bob Aiese

Printed in the United States of America

Library of Congress Cataloging-in-Publication Data

Adatto, Leslie
Roof Explorer's Guide: 101 New York City Rooftops / by Leslie Adatto;
photographs by Heather Shimmin and Ari Burling

ISBN 978-0-9960036-0-5

Additional photo credits:
Pages 34-35, 196-197 Rhea Alexander,
pages 184-185 Sharokh Mirzai,
pages 174-175, 200-201 Arlene Bender
plus contributions as noted.

Published by Leslie Adatto
338 W. 11th Street, #3A
New York, NY 10014
leslie@roofsnyc.com

To Laura M. Brown, Ph.D.,
who, all those years ago,
introduced me to New York City,
the love of my life.

p. 22 PH-D Rooftop Lounge

p. 110 Elevated Acre

p. 174 Riverbank State Park

LE BAIN

CONTENTS

Section 1: 10-67
Hotel Rooftop Bars, Restaurants and More

Section 2: 68-105
Rooftop Bars and Restaurants

Section 3: 106-125
Elevated Parks

Section 4: 126-163
Museums, Theaters and Green Roofs

Section 5: 164-187
Elevated Farms

Section 6: 188-219
Rooftop Classes, Entertainment and Sports

Suggested Itineraries 220-221

Index 222-224

INTRODUCTION

Get ready to experience New York City from an entirely fresh perspective – from the rooftops! *Roof Explorer's Guide:101 New York City Rooftops* is the only guide book that shows you - and guides you to - a wondrous variety of exciting New York City rooftops.

Go to trendy bars and restaurants, take a swim or play some tennis, attend a movie, go to a farm, visit 19th-century historical sites, check out a museum or a play, or snooze on a park bench, all on New York City rooftops.

I'm Leslie Adatto, the New York City roof explorer. I have discovered hundreds of rooftops throughout the City's five boroughs, and in this book I share 101 of my favorites with you. *Roof Explorer's Guide: 101 New York City Rooftops* gives veteran New Yorkers and visitors alike my personal know-how to explore a huge variety of New York City rooftops.

I hope the photography and information throughout this book will inspire you to venture out and experience New York City in this thrilling new way.

How to use this guide

Roof Explorer's Guide is divided into six easy-to-use sections. The first two sections cover rooftop bars and restaurants. Sections 3 and 4 include elevated parks, museums and green roofs. Section 5 explores rooftop farms, and Section 6 delves into rooftop entertainment and sports.

Within each section, listings are organized geographically, starting at the bottom of Manhattan and heading uptown, then to Brooklyn, Queens, the Bronx and Staten Island.

All 101 rooftops included in this book are places that you can visit, just like I did. Some might require a little advanced planning, some are open seasonally and a few are open just one or two days a year, but all are accessible to urban roof explorers just like us.

The sidebars next to each listing will give you the detailed information you need to plan your visit.

You may want to visit rooftops listed in different sections that are close by one another so I have included some suggested itineraries (p. 220-221) that allow you to do your own mini-tours of New York rooftops.

Since this book includes rooftops all over New York City, you may need various modes of transportation when exploring. While most of the roofs are easily accessible by walking, subway, buses and cabs, the vast majority of my personal roof exploring was done by bicycle. For those determined to see as many rooftops as possible in the shortest amount of time, I recommend taking advantage of Citi Bikes (citibikesnyc.com) or day-long bike rentals (bikenewyorkcity.com or bikeshopny.com). Very rarely, you'll need a ferry and/or a car to explore the most outlying New York City rooftops.

Keeping in touch

There are several ways to keep in touch about our ongoing exploration of New York City rooftops. Make sure to visit the Roof Explorer's Guide website (roofexplorersguide. com) for updated information, subscribe to my blog (lookingupwithleslie.com) for rooftop stories and event coverage, and visit my Facebook page where I post relevant articles about rooftops in New York City and everywhere (facebook.com/lookingupwithleslie).

Plus, we can continue to explore together. When you come across a new rooftop, or a rooftop event, please share this exciting information with me via my website (roofexplorersguide.com). Finally, I'd be thrilled if you would share, via the same website, your personal experiences as you discover 101 New York City Rooftops.

LA PISCINE

New York City is rediscovering its valuable rooftop real estate, and hotels are leading the charge! Savvy hotel owners understand the allure of an al fresco rooftop cocktail, often with a fabulous view, and have capitalized on it in dozens of properties throughout Manhattan, Brooklyn, Queens and Staten Island.

Visit the ultra-swanky Salon de Ning atop the historic Peninsula Hotel on posh Fifth Avenue, the Ides Bar at the repurposed Wythe Hotel in hipster Williamsburg, The Jimmy's newly constructed rooftop pool and lounge at the James Hotel in artsy SoHo, and dozens of other varied hotel rooftop bars that each offer a different vibe and view.

SECTION 1:

HOTEL ROOFTOP BARS, RESTAURANTS AND MORE

1. LOOPY DOOPY ROOFTOP BAR AT THE CONRAD HOTEL

Named after an eye-popping 80 x 100 foot Sol LeWitt painting installed in the 13-floor atrium lobby of this luxurious contemporary hotel, Loopy Doopy is an intimate, trendy rooftop bar. The background music is well chosen and modulated to inspire unparalleled sunset watching over New York Harbor and the Statue of Liberty with a creative, well-crafted summer cocktail in hand. As Loopy Doopy is the first American bar to have prosecco on tap, their signature drink is the Boozy Icepop served in a champagne glass. Note that the mint in the mojito and the greens served with the shrimp cocktail are grown just feet away in the rooftop chef's garden, just out of sight, above and behind the bar. The 65-person capacity bar is wide open, so if you're up there watching the boats ferry tourists to Liberty Island during daytime hours, remember your hat and sunglasses. Although the Loopy Doopy primarily serves the after-work crowd and tourists staying in the hotel, it's a great stop after a movie at the multiplex downstairs or when enjoying the beauty of Battery Park City.

Loopy Doopy Rooftop Bar

Location: Battery Park City

Address: 102 North End Ave. NY, NY 10281

Phone: 646.769.4250

conradnewyork.com/ loopydoopy

Subway:

Subway Stop: 1 to Cortland St. or E to World Trade Center

Calendar: May-Oct

Hours: Mon–Thu 4pm-1am, Fri 4pm–1am, Sat noon– 1am, Sun noon–midnight

$$$

Photos courtesy of Loopy Doopy Bar

2. BAR D'EAU
AT THE TRUMP SOHO NEW YORK

An elegant treasure hides on the seventh floor setback of the Trump SoHo, a spacious and uncrowded poolside cocktail bar and restaurant that opened in the neighborhood's tallest building in 2010.

This seasonal terrace has three private cabanas plus plenty of seating around the pool/waterfalls. You'll find more seating near the only rooftop bocce court I've come across. While the pool is for hotel guests, the bocce court is open to rooftop drinkers. The bar's good neighbor policy means an early closing time, between 9 and 10 p.m. each night.

Maybe it's not packed full of people because of its location in an emerging neighborhood that, until recently, was struggling with its identity. Sandwiched in between SoHo to the east, Greenwich Village to the north and TriBeCa to the south, the area recently christened "Hudson Square" was formerly known as the "Printing District." It continues to be home to many media-related businesses, and now boasts a thriving art community as well. So if you're looking for a quiet outdoor drink in an elegant setting, visit Bar D'Eau soon because, as the reputation of Hudson Square grows, this sleepy, elegant rooftop bar may well be "discovered."

Bar d'Eau

Location: Hudson Square / SoHo West

Address: 246 Spring St. NY, NY 10013

Phone: 212.842.5500

trumphotelcollection.com/soho/soho-bars.php

Subway:

Ⓒ Ⓔ ① ②

Subway Stop:C/E to Spring St. or 1/2 to Canal or Houston

Calendar: May-Sept

Hours: 11am-10pm

$$$

Photos courtesy of Bar d' Eau

15

Jimmy

Location: SoHo

Address: 15 Thompson St. NY, NY 10013

Phone: 212.201.9118

jimmysoho.com

Subway:

Subway Stop: Canal St.

Calendar: Year-round in the evening. Jun-Sept open at noon

Hours: Sun-Wed 5pm–1am, Thu–Sat 5pm–2am. During summer, Sat and Sun open at noon

$$$

Photo courtesy of Jimmy

3. JIMMY AT THE JAMES HOTEL

So what if it's a 26-degree night in January? Year-round, you can hang out poolside at Jimmy, 18 floors above SoHo, sipping a Mexican Bee Hive (silver tequila, honey, lavender syrup, lime juice and a real chunk of amber honeycomb), or other inventive cocktails, some delightfully fashioned with herbs grown a few floors down in one of the hotel's elevated gardens. From one of the highest rooftop bars in trendy SoHo, enjoy unobstructed views of lower Manhattan that stretch east, south and west.

When it's chilly out, winter guests can step inside to warm up in the lounge, but for warm weather visitors, the splash-sized pool is adorned with magnificent iridescent tiles that make it the jewel in the crown of this modern, upscale, fashionable bar. Summertime dips in the pool can be followed by a rinse in one of the outdoor showers and sun- or moon-bathing on the hip, minimalist lounge furniture.

4. SOAKED AT THE MONDRIAN SOHO

This 26th floor penthouse presidential suite turned rooftop bar feels like you've been invited to a very wealthy friend's swanky private roof party (albeit with a cash bar). With a maximum capacity of 200 (and that would be tight), this is an intimate rooftop venue.

In keeping with the swanky New York private party vibe, the crowd is casual but definitely trendy and attractive, so dress accordingly. The creative cocktails are made with organic fruits, very little sugar and no artificial flavors.

Atop the tallest building in SoHo, Soaked offers unrivaled views of downtown Manhattan, and some pretty spectacular uptown vistas as well. Sunset into nighttime, this panorama cannot be beat. Open seasonally and only five days a week in good weather, this destination should be at the top of your list on a warm summer evening.

Soaked

Location: SoHo close to Chinatown

Address: 150 Lafayette St. NY, NY 10013

Phone: 212.389.1000

soakedsoho.com

Subway:

Ⓙ Ⓩ Ⓝ Ⓠ ⑥

Subway Stop: Canal St.

Calendar: Jun-Sept

Hours: Open Wed-Sun, weather permitting. Wed and Thur/Sun 6pm-12:30am, Fri and Sat 4pm-12:30am

Reservations: Recommended

$$$

Photos courtesy of Soaked

5. LE BAIN AT THE STANDARD, HIGH LINE

The 180-degree views from the 19th floor rooftop of the Standard Hotel give visitors the sensation of cruising up the Hudson River on the top deck of a ship, watching Manhattan floating by. Once you establish that you are indeed on terra firma (or almost 200 feet above it), the charms of the field turf covered rooftop with cushy seating and a casual atmosphere instantly wash over you. The summery drinks are served by the glass, or in pitchers to share with friends, the crêperie serves wonderful snacks, and the sunsets are stunning. Stationary telescopes are provided for more detailed city, river and New Jersey viewing.

Le Bain

Location: Meatpacking District

Address: 444 W. 13th St. NY, NY 10014

Phone: 212.645.4646

standardhotels.com/high-line

Subway:

Ⓛ Ⓐ Ⓒ Ⓔ

Subway Stop: L to Eighth Ave. or A/C/E to 14th St.

Calendar: Weather permitting

Hours: Open daily Mon 4pm-midnight, Tue and Wed 4pm-4am, Thu-Sat 2pm-4am and Sun 2pm-3am

Reservations: Suggested

$$$

Photos courtesy of Le Bain

21

PH-D Rooftop Lounge

Location: Meatpacking District

Address: 355 W. 16th St. NY, NY 10011

Phone: 212.229.2511

phdlounge.com

Subway:

Subway Stop: A/C/E to 14th St, L to Eighth Ave, 1 to 18th St.

Calendar: Year-round

Hours: Mon-Sat 5pm-4am and Sun 5pm-9pm

Reservations: Required for groups

$$$

Photo by Heather Shimmin

6. PH-D ROOFTOP LOUNGE AT THE DREAM DOWNTOWN

Situated in a cluster of Meatpacking District rooftop bars, PH-D Rooftop Lounge exudes a distinctly Vegas-nightclub vibe. The late-night weekend crowd is young, trendy and beautiful, happy with loud electronic dance mixes played by DJs on an impressive sound system, and accustomed to guest lists, bottle service, waiting on line behind velvet ropes and choosey doormen. This club really gets going around 1 a.m. on Friday and Saturday nights. Be young, dress to impress and have plenty of money to spend, and you're sure to have a fabulous time.

For the more mature crowd, arrive early at this 12th floor rooftop lounge and grab one of the comfortable, private banquettes in the leafy outdoor terrace. You will be rewarded with a stunning northward Manhattan skyline view, including the Empire State Building. So whether you're young and trendy, or stylishly mature, the terrace at PH-D Rooftop Lounge is a great place to unwind with a sunset or evening skyline view cocktail.

7. GRAMERCY TERRACE
AT THE GRAMERCY PARK HOTEL

Lexington Avenue ends at E. 21st Street, where it runs into gated and locked Gramercy Park. Right next to this elegant private park with the coveted keys is the storied Gramercy Park Hotel, an 18-story Renaissance Revival Style structure built in 1924. In 1926, Humphrey Bogart married his first wife on the rooftop of this legendary hotel, and today you can have breakfast, lunch or brunch on the same rooftop.

The Gramercy Park Hotel, known for its bohemian charm, hosted guests ranging from a young JFK lodging with his parents, to reggae music legend Bob Marley, to the punk band the Clash. Babe Ruth was a regular at the bar in the 1930s. David Mamet, Madonna and Bob Dylan also frequented this hub of high bohemia.

After falling into disrepair, the hotel reopened in 2006 when Ian Schrager and Julian Schnabel restyled it from bottom to top, including the 18th floor roof garden restaurant, Gramercy Terrace. In contrast to the eclectic lobby that is dominated by an enormous wood-burning fireplace and an impressive art collection, Gramercy Terrace is full of natural light and, when it's warm enough to retract the roof, cool breezes. Combining casual elegance, excellent food and a welcoming atmosphere, Gramercy Terrace draws a large local crowd to its hotel rooftop. The Danny Meyer menu offers superbly made and presented comfort food, such as the deliciously decadent Bread Pudding French Toast served with sweet cream and berries. Service is friendly and efficient. The sofas, tables and chairs are arranged so the casual yet stylish diners can enjoy a private conversation if they so choose. Views are limited when the rooftop is closed during colder weather but, year-round, enough sunlight streams through the cheerful greenery to cure a mild case of the winter blues.

Gramercy Terrace

Location: Gramercy

Address: 2 Lexington Ave. NY, NY 10010 between E. 21st and E. 22nd St.

Phone: 212.201.2171

gramercyterrace.com

Subway:

6

Subway Stop: 23rd St.

Calendar: Year-round

Hours: 7am-11am for breakfast and 11am-3pm for lunch daily. Brunch 11am-3pm Sat and Sun

Reservations: Strongly suggested

$$$

Photo courtesy of Gramercy Terrace

8. LA PISCINE AT THE HÔTEL AMERICANO

Take the glass-enclosed elevator directly from the street to this tenth floor rooftop oozing with sophisticated Latin flare. La Piscine, named for its amusingly small rooftop swimming pool, is the bar and restaurant atop the boutique Hôtel Americano, designed by the famous Mexican architect, Enrique Norten. Looking over the High Line in fashion model-saturated industrial Chelsea, La Piscine also offers a majestic view of the Empire State Building and a slice of the Hudson wide enough to enjoy watching the sun sink below the river. Warm weather guests can dip in the pool, then rinse off in one of the two outdoor showers while swaying to the beat of a Latin-themed musical playlist personally selected by Bebel Gilberto. During cooler months, the small pool becomes a large hot tub, and guests are supplied with plush robes and towels to keep cozy. The Grill at La Piscine offers a scaled down, grilled-before-your-eyes Mediterranean style menu that makes you feel like a guest at a posh friend's home barbeque. Choose from eight mezcals and numerous Blanco, Añejo or Resposado tequilas at the bar that also features beer, wine and champagne. Plus, this is one rooftop bar where you can glimpse the July Fourth fireworks for as long as Macy's keeps their world-famous display over the Hudson River.

La Piscine

Location: Chelsea

Address: 518 W. 27th St. NY, NY 10001

Phone: 212.525.0000

hotel-americano.com

Subway:

Subway Stop: C/E to 23rd St. or 1 to 28th St.

Calendar: Year-round

Hours: Opens May-Sept Fri, Sat and Sun noon, the rest of the time from 5pm

Reservations: Strongly suggested

$$$-$$$$

Photos courtesy of La Piscine

9. GANSEVOORT PARK ROOFTOP AT GANSEVOORT PARK HOTEL

Be prepared to get past the discriminating doormen before being invited to enter the elevator to the 20th and 21st penthouse floors that house the tri-level Gansevoort Park Rooftop. Push P1 and be whisked away to the 20th floor Main Bar, a backlit beauty embellished with sexy artwork under a glamorous chandelier. The long terrace offers outdoor seating, perfect in warm weather. But when it's cold out, enjoy the city view from the lounge seating through the Main Bar's floor-to-ceiling windows, or look around this people-watchers' paradise.

Pushing P2 delivers you to the Pool Bar and the indoor/outdoor pool/lounge area. While the heated pool is reserved for hotel guests, it serves as a fun centerpiece, embellished with a pool-bottom mosaic of a classic 1940s pinup girl. The elaborate outdoor sound system brings the nightly danceable deejay music poolside where it feels like you can reach out and almost touch the top 30 floors of the Empire State Building or the massive golden rooftop that crowns the Credit Suisse Building (the former Met Life Building) in nearby Madison Square Park.

Private event rooms abound in this 20,000 square foot, tri-level "entertainment complex." Those who reserve the P2-level "Blue Room" can warm themselves by its outdoor fireplace. The "Red Room" has its own outdoor terrace.

A final ascent to the Gansevoort Park's top most level is The Sundeck, a completely outdoor space open only during summer.

Gansevoort Park Rooftop

Location: Flatiron District

Address: 420 Park Ave South. NY, NY 10016

Phone: 212.317.2900

gansevoortparkrooftop.com

Subway:

Subway Stop: 28th St.

Calendar: Year-round

Hours: 6pm-4am weekends and from 6pm-2am weeknights

Reservations: Recommended

$$$

Photo courtesy of Gansevoort Park Rooftop

Location: Herald Square

Address: 71 W. 35th St
18th Floor, NY, NY 10001

Phone: 212.630.9993

addisongroupnyc.com/
venues/monarch/

Subway:

B D F M
N Q R

Subway Stop: 34th St.-
Herald Square

Calendar: Year-round

Hours: Sun-Thu 3pm-2am,
Fri and Sat 3pm-4am

Reservations:
Recommended but walk-ins
are welcome based on
capacity

$$$

Photo courtesy of
Monarch Rooftop

10. MONARCH ROOFTOP ATOP THE COURTYARD BY MARRIOTT (HERALD SQUARE)

You enter on the ground floor through the completely utilitarian lobby at the Courtyard by Marriott, but with a quick elevator ride, you enter the extravagant fabulousness of the indoor-outdoor Monarch Rooftop. Named after the "king of butterflies," the Monarch Rooftop offers the casual, adult crowd a wrap-around terrace with comfortable couches, topiary trees, and two completely distinct and outstanding views. The art-deco Empire State Building is so close to the Monarch Rooftop you feel you could flit right over. The second and equally spectacular view is around the corner, extending seemingly forever up and down Sixth Avenue, also known as Avenue of the Americas.

It is no surprise that several of the cocktail list's signature creations are named after butterflies: The Fiery Skipper, the Duskywing, the Firetip and the American Lady. A light fare menu is also offered, plus, something not commonly found on Manhattan roof lounges: Specialty chocolate desserts and coffee. This makes Monarch a great place to continue the party with butterfly-inspired cocktails, or to relax above it all with a sinfully indulgent sweet and cup of java.

11. REFINERY ROOFTOP AT THE REFINERY HOTEL

More stylish than its surroundings, Refinery Rooftop offers a luxury rooftop bar and lounge in a transitioning neighborhood. This newest addition to the Manhattan elevated hotel bar collection is striving to attract the business-chic clientele, so leave the shorts and flip flops at home (or in your hotel room if you are lucky enough to be staying at this hip boutique hotel).

Exiting the hotel, you encounter an indoor oasis sporting a fireplace, a stone fountain and a DJ with a stellar sound system. Next is the bar area with terra cotta tiles and a gorgeous retractable glass rooftop, open in lovely weather but affording you the rooftop experience without getting wet or chilled when Mother Nature is not cooperative. And when it's perfect outside, Refinery Rooftop offers guests a perfect outdoor space. Wood decking, potted roses, porch swings, and cushioned sofas and club chairs create a luxe patio ambience. Cocktails are fresh and creative, and the rooftop bar menu offers delicious small plates. Plus, the enormous Empire State Building, just four blocks away, feels so close you might think you could invite it to your table and order it a drink.

Refinery Rooftop

Location: Midtown near Herald Square

Address: 63 W. 38th St. New York, NY 10018

Phone: 212-729-0277

refineryrooftopnyc.com

Subway:

B D F M N Q R

Subway Stop: 34th St.-Herald Square

Calendar: Year-round

Hours: Open daily 5pm-1am

Reservations: Recommended by email 24 hours in advance, walk-ins welcome based on capacity

$$$

Photo courtesy of Refinery Rooftop

12. ROOFTOP AT POD 39 HOTEL

The only Northern Italian Renaissance style rooftop bar in New York City, this delightful nearly century-old rooftop has been reimagined by the hip restaurateur, Ken Friedman, as a Mexican hacienda with a cabana-like bar set among the original Greco-Roman style brick arches and terra-cotta columns. Seventeen floors up, this casual rooftop offers cooling East River breezes (and partial views) on a hot evening. On cooler nights, The Rooftop brings out heaters, allowing for the early start of their roof season in April or May, and the late closing in October or November, in contrast to many other New York City rooftops that don't open until late May and close in mid-September.

Ivy grows up the weathered brick walls, near the potted roses and mint, and strings of white lights add to the festive ambiance. The cocktail list continues the Mexican-holiday vibe, made with jalapeno-infused rum, or cinnamon-vanilla bean, or served in a glass rimmed with chili salt. "The Watermelon" is made with the spirit of your choice, watermelon puree, lime and agave nectar served in an actual baby watermelon. Order guacamole and chips on the rooftop, or bring up "takeout" from the fabulous Salvation Taco downstairs. I highly recommend the cauliflower tacos.

Rooftop at Pod 39

Location: Murray Hill

Address: 145 E 39th St.
NY, NY 10016

Phone: 212.865.5700

thepodhotel.com

Subway:

4 5 6 7 S

Subway Stop: 42nd St.-
Grand Central

Calendar: Seasonal

Hours: Open daily Apr-Nov
(depending on weather)
5pm-2am

$$-$$$

Photo by Rhea Alexander

Bookmarks

Location: Midtown East

Address: 299 Madison Ave.
NY, NY 10017 at E. 41st St.

Phone: 212.204.5498

libraryhotel.com

Subway:

Subway Stop: 42nd St.-
Grand Central

Calendar: Year-round

Hours: Mon-Fri 4pm-
midnight, Sat 5pm-1am and
Sun 5pm-midnight

$$$

Photos courtesy of
Bookmarks

13. BOOKMARKS AT THE LIBRARY HOTEL

When you want to know what it feels like to have an elegant Midtown penthouse apartment with a small, wraparound terrace, visit Bookmarks Lounge.

From Bookmarks, the 14th floor indoor/outdoor rooftop lounge of the hushed Library Hotel (what else would a hotel calling itself "Library" be?), peer over the charming brick detailed parapet wall and look straight into the magnificent Fifth Avenue entrance of the New York Public Library, where Patience and Fortitude, the two lion statues flanking the entrance steps, welcome all book lovers. From this vantage point 150 feet above E. 41st Street, it also becomes obvious that the New York Public Library, and Bryant Park right behind it, are not on the "grid," the 1811 street plan that delineates the vast majority of Manhattan above 14th Street. What can't be seen from the rooftop terrace at Bookmarks is that in the exact spot where the majestic New York Public Library now stands was a four-acre man-made lake called the Croton Reservoir that supplied fresh water to Manhattanites until the early 20th century, when its replacement was built in the middle of Central Park.

A quiet, but definitely not hushed, hotel bar, Bookmarks has background music just loud enough to provide atmosphere, but not too loud to have a conversation. Outdoor space is at a premium. The two cozy outdoor areas provide views of the surrounding taller midtown office buildings, and at night, looking west, guests can see the lighted spires atop the Bank of America and New York Times buildings.

Indoors, Bookmarks provides a cozy fireplace, club chairs and comfy couches. On the way to the charming open-air back terrace, you pass through a covered, heated solarium with wicker tables and chairs, which is a great place to stop when the weather decides not to cooperate. The front terrace, also surrounded by the charming brick parapet wall, is covered and heated during winter.

14. SKY ROOM AT FAIRFIELD INN AND SUITES MARRIOTT TIMES SQUARE

This Hell's Kitchen rooftop lounge reflects the changes the Times Square tourist mecca continues to undergo. Situated just across from the Port Authority bus terminal, the street-level entrance to the Sky Room briefly exposes you to the grittier side of Manhattan. The lobby is a bit of a throwback as well, with garish chandeliers and reflective wall tiles.

Yet like so many New York establishments, this book should not be judged by its cover. The doormen require "business casual" attire for admittance, and, ladies, this is the place to wear your highest heels and most fabulous party dresses.

A year-round destination, three indoor areas are designed

Sky Room

Location: Hell's Kitchen

Address: 330 W. 40th St. NY, NY 10018

Phone: 212.380.1195

skyroomnyc.com

Subway:

Ⓐ Ⓒ Ⓔ

Subway Stop: 42nd St.-Port Authority

Calendar: Year-round

Hours: Open Mon-Sat 5pm-4am, during summer Sundays 5pm-4am

Reservations: Recommended

$$-$$$

Photos courtesy of Sky Room

with a stylized nod to the colorful chaos of the nearby Times Square neon and traffic. The two outdoor lounges are the real draw, however.

Thirty-four floors above the Hell's Kitchen grunge is the thin ribbon called the North Terrace. It overlooks Times Square and has low-slung couches, a full bar, a DJ booth and a retractable glass roof. Through a narrow passageway is the South Terrace, offering private cabanas and sliver views of the Hudson River and Empire State Building.

The best food and drink deals on a NYC hotel rooftop bar are found at Sky Room's happy hour, every Tuesday-Friday from 5-8 p.m. Plus at this time of day, it's easier to get a seat on one of the couches or in a cabana. Late night, there is a cover charge and mandatory coat check, and drinks and bottle service prices almost as high as this 34th floor lounge.

The Terrace at YOTEL

Location: Hell's Kitchen/
Theater District

Address: 570 Tenth Ave.
NY, NY 10036

Phone: 646.449.7700

yotel.com/Hotels/New-York-
City/EAT-DRINK

Subway:

Subway Stop: 42nd St.-
Port Authority

Calendar: Year-round,
weather permitting

Hours: Open daily 7am-1am

$$-$$$

Photos courtesy of The
Terrace at YOTEL

15. THE TERRACE AT YOTEL NEW YORK

A study in contrasts: YOTEL has built its fun, youthful and hip reputation by offering ultra-efficient, compact rooms, some of the smallest in a city known for small hotel rooms, yet it boasts Manhattan's largest outdoor hotel terrace. This disparity makes perfect sense for the young population YOTEL attracts. A private room is merely for sleeping and showering, but New York City is for partying with friends and strangers, and The Terrace at YOTEL provides plenty of room to do just that.

Carrying on the hotel's futuristic, Japanese inspired design, The Terrace is thoughtfully furnished with distinctly modern modular furniture, some spaces designed for couples and others for groups. Two full bars and friendly, efficient staff make sure you have all the Asian-inspired drinks (sake sangria, how original!) and eats as you want, so you can stay awhile to enjoy the changing vista. The afternoon views from this fourth floor rooftop terrace are distinctly New York City, and happy hour is Monday-Friday from 4-7 p.m. As you nurse the last of your happy hour cocktail, while the sun sets and the lights and skyscraper spires of the Theater District buildings begin to glow, afternoon into evening on The Terrace becomes even more spectacular.

16. HENRY'S ROOFTOP BAR AT THE ROGER SMITH HOTEL

If staying at the art-centric Roger Smith Hotel begs the question, "Who is Roger Smith?," then heading up to the open-air patio bar on the 16th floor, Henry's Rooftop Bar, makes one wonder, "Who the heck is Henry?"

After some digging around, I discovered the hotel was named after an "everyman" traveler, Roger Smith, seeking adventure and creative inspiration in the Big Apple. It turns out that Henry, however, is not a spirit but a very corporeal Boston terrier, the hotel's resident mascot.

While a definite improvement over popping open a Rolling Rock beer on your own fire escape, Henry's is a casual, small (a crowd of 35 fills up the place), unpretentious rooftop bar with a nice string of lights and just a few modest planters providing a small splash of greenery. From this midtown rooftop a glimpse of the Chrysler Building is on offer, but most don't come for the view or the "scene." They come for a convivial, affordable, outdoor gathering spot, and a casual respite from the hustle and bustle of Midtown to relax or meet friends. Henry's is the perfect place for an after-work beer or maybe even a well-made caipirinha, Brazil's national cocktail, the house specialty.

Henry's Rooftop Bar

Location: Midtown East

Address: 501 Lexington Ave. NY, NY 10017 at E. 47th St.

Phone: 212.755.1400

rogersmith.com

Subway:

④ ⑤ ⑥ ⑦

Subway Stop: 42nd St.- Grand Central

Calendar: Memorial Day-Oct

Hours: Mon-Sat 5pm-10pm

$$

Photos by Heather Shimmin

The Press Lounge

Location: Western edge of Hell's Kitchen

Address: 653 Eleventh Ave. NY, NY 10036

Phone: 212.757.2224

thepresslounge.com

Subway:

C E

Subway Stop: 50th St. (then a 10-minute walk)

Best way to get there: Subway or the M11 bus

Calendar: Year-round

Hours: Sun-Tue 5pm-1am, Wed-Sat 5pm-2am

Reservations: Recommended

$$$-$$$$

Photo by Ari Burling

17. THE PRESS LOUNGE AT INK 48 HOTEL

Leave your cares 16 floors below when you step out of the express elevator into The Press Lounge. This expansive, elegant rooftop bar offers 360-degree Manhattan views and comfortable couches where you're encouraged to relax with a well-made cocktail in hand. Begin with sunset views over the Hudson, then turn east and let the lighted spires, theaters and streets of Midtown dazzle you. As you look north and south, the red glow of brake lights streaming along Eleventh Avenue seems infinite.

At 8,500 square feet, The Press Lounge is large enough to have four distinct areas. The indoor area, The Press Lounge proper, offers comfortable leather couches, 20-foot floor-to-ceiling windows and unobtrusive ambient music. The immediately adjacent Rooftop Garden has open-air seating during warmer months, and when it's cooler, an enclosure of retractable clear plastic walls and couches equipped with plush blankets. The year-round open air space, The Press Lounge North Side, features a 20-foot long reflecting pool surrounded by mid-century modern-esque egg-shaped wicker furniture. Finally, The Greenhouse, designated for private parties from 2 to 25 people, is only accessible with advance planning. Originally a hot tub, this glassed-in area overlooks the Hudson, and has been transformed into a recessed outdoor dining room surrounded by a compact container rooftop farm where the chef's favorite herbs are grown. If you expect your La Caravelle Brut Rose champagne to be served in a crystal fluted glass, be warned: The Press Lounge complies with New York City law that requires outdoor venues to use plastic barware, even when serving a $23 glass of bubbly.

18. AVA LOUNGE AT THE DREAM HOTEL

When it's time to take a break from dancing or shouting over the loud deejay music that fills the 15th floor indoor lounge, carry your carefully crafted cocktail up the narrow flight of stairs to the Miami-inspired outdoor rooftop at the Ava Lounge. Hang out with the fashionable crowd while enjoying the sunset and then the spectacular Theater District lights at this cozy beach-holiday style rooftop.

Earlier in the week and earlier in the evening, gaining entrance to this chic bar is a snap, but an hour or two before midnight, especially on warm summer Fridays and Saturdays, expect to wait on the ground floor behind the velvet rope. When the doorman allows you into one of the narrow elevators, it opens into the bar's hallway entrance that is adorned with scintillating black and white photographs. Available year-round, the indoor bar offers lovely views through its large windows, but the open-air, beachy rooftop is set up for guests only during summer months.

Ava Lounge
Location: Midtown West

Address: 210 W. 55th St. NY, NY 10019, between Seventh Ave. and Broadway

Phone: 212.956.7020

avaloungenyc.com

Subway:

Ⓝ Ⓠ Ⓡ Ⓑ Ⓓ Ⓔ

Subway Stop: N/Q/R to 57th St, or B/D or E to Seventh Ave.

Calendar: Mid-May through mid-Oct

Hours: Mon-Wed 4pm-3am, Thu-Sat 4pm-4am and Sun 4pm-2am

Reservations: Recommended

$$$

Photo by Ari Burling

47

19. AKA CENTRAL PARK HOTEL

Sleep where Diane Keaton, Jennifer Lawrence and Richie Sambora of Bon Jovi have slept – under the stars - when you reserve the Outdoor Bedroom at AKA Central Park. From mid-May through mid-October, guests who book one of the two 17th floor penthouses can have the king size bed moved onto the 1,000 square-foot private wrap-around terrace. Gaze across at the Plaza Hotel from between 400-count Frette sheets and a matching duvet. A telescope for stargazing (and I don't mean Plaza Hotel guest stargazing!) is included, as are other romance-inducing amenities: a wood-burning fireplace, champagne, chocolate covered strawberries, a sound system and an e-reader already loaded with romantic poetry selections, candles and flowers. If you can tear yourself away from the luxurious penthouse, upper Fifth Avenue is home to nine world-class museums, including the Metropolitan Museum of Art (where the Cantor Roof Garden is open from May through November), MoMA, and the Frank Lloyd Wright-designed Guggenheim.

Just one block from Central Park and a shopaholic's heartbeat away from Bergdorf Goodman and Tiffany's flagship store, this location above the heart of New York City offers roof explorers with deep pockets a once-in-a-lifetime experience.

AKA Central Park

Location: Midtown

Address: 42 W. 58th St. NY, NY 10019, near Fifth Ave.

Phone: 212.753.3500

hotelaka.com

Subway:

N Q R

Subway Stop: 59th St.

Calendar: May-Oct

Reservations: Required

$$$$$

Photo courtesy of AKA Central Park

20. SKY TERRACE AT HUDSON HOTEL

Once you've finally made it to the Sky Terrace, relax and stay a while! It's a bit of journey, up the escalator to the lobby, then left to the elevators to the 15th floor, then left again down the narrow hallway until you find the door marked "Sky Terrace."

This sophisticated, inviting wrap-around terrace wends through a myriad of semi-private seating areas, offering rooftop visitors a choice of cushioned sun beds, day-beds strewn with colorful pillows that are big enough for two, tables and bistro chairs and one very coveted oversized hammock. From this 15th floor oasis, you have south-facing city and west-facing river views, and this high up, even on a hot summer day, the breeze is cool. Lots of ivy, large trees, flowering shrubs and even some edibles give Sky Terrace a very resort-like ambience that makes the streets of New York City, just 150 feet below, seem miles away. In the evening, to mirror the glamorous city lights, romantic lanterns light the walkways.

A menu that includes 10 variations on sangria, cocktails, wine and beer is on offer, but food isn't. When you get hungry, head down to the trendy second floor outdoor space, Tequila Park, adjacent to the lobby, and order some terrific tacos. You'll still be on a rooftop – disguised as an outdoor courtyard - just not quite as high up.

Sky Terrace is the perfect place to gather for quiet conversation, or even to spend time alone, especially if you can snag time in the hammock! The music plays just in the background and the bar closes relatively early, so those looking for a late night party atmosphere may want to start here but end their night elsewhere.

Sky Terrace

Location: Hell's Kitchen/ Midtown West

Address: 356 W. 58th St. NY, NY 10019, between Eighth and Ninth Ave.

Phone: 212.554.6000

morganhotelgroup.com/ Hudson/Hudson-newyork/ eat-drink/sky-terrace

Subway:

 A C B D 1

Subway Stop: 59th St.- Columbus Circle

Calendar: May-Sept

Hours: 8am-10pm

$$$

Photo courtesy of Sky Terrace

Salon de Ning

Location: Midtown

Address: 700 Fifth Ave. NY, NY 10019 at 55th St.

Phone: 212.903.3097

newyork.peninsula.com

Subway:

Subway Stop:53rd St.-Fifth Ave.

Calendar: Year-round weather permitting

Hours: Mon-Sat 5pm-1am and Sun 5pm-midnight

$$$$

Photo courtesy of Salon de Ning

21. SALON DE NING AT THE PENINSULA HOTEL

Salon de Ning's Asian influences echo their famous sister hotel, the Peninsula Hong Kong. The 23rd floor sophisticated lounge surrounds you in dark woods and seductive, tasteful décor. Stylish and casually dressy, Salon de Ning is perfectly suited to the renowned hotel it crowns. The well-heeled or those looking to meet the well-heeled frequent this elegant rooftop with stunning views up and down the most famous section of Fifth Avenue, above the parade of elegant shops and other five-star New York hotels.

From the north terrace of Salon de Ning, see something only the privileged few who live or work in high-rises nearby ever get to see: The award-winning Ken Smith-designed rooftop of MoMA's sixth floor gallery, and a view from above of the spectacular Rachel Whiteread "Water Tower" (1998), a light-catching resin cast of an actual cedar water tower, perched on another elevation of MoMA's rooftop. Tuck binoculars into your Prada bag, as you will be seventeen floors above these two exceptional works of art that even your MoMA membership card will not show you.

Location: Lincoln Center

Address: 44 W. 63rd St.
near Broadway

Phone: 212.265.7400

empirehotelnyc.com

Subway:

Subway Stop: 1 to 66th St.
or A/C/ B/D or 1 to 59th St.-
Columbus Circle

Calendar: Year-round for
The Rooftop; May-Sept for
The Pool Deck

Hours: Rooftop 5pm-3am
on weekends, earlier during
the week. Pool Deck 10am-
10pm from Memorial Day-
Labor Day

Reservations: Suggested

$$-$$$$

Photos courtesy of The
Rooftop at the Empire Hotel

22. THE ROOFTOP AND THE POOL DECK AT THE EMPIRE HOTEL

The Empire Hotel, across from Lincoln Center, has three rooftops that each offer unique experiences, all depending on how much you are willing to spend. On The Rooftop, 12 floors up, listen to live jazz on a Monday night and take advantage of the happy hour drinks specials before 8 p.m. You can enjoy the Upper West Side views over Central Park and Lincoln Center and have a satisfying rooftop experience under the retro glow of the red neon Empire sign for a song. After 8, it's prudent to make reservations for The Rooftop as the lines get longer as the evening gets later, especially on the weekends, and wanna-be partiers are sometimes turned away. Oddly enough, the length of the elevator line doesn't always determine how crowded it is at the bar. Be warned: Bottle service and loud music make this roof bar a weekend party destination.

Between Memorial Day and Labor Day, you can up the ante, get a room and gain access to the 150-person capacity Pool Deck with its plunge pool and sun beds. For those with cash to spare who want the most deluxe rooftop experience the Empire Hotel has to offer, reserve a private cabana with an iPod docking station, plasma screen TV, a personal refrigerator and free wireless internet ($75 for a half day, $150 for a full day) on the rooftop steps below the pool. Drinks and limited food are available as well, plus, if you feel the need to unwind even further, you can arrange for an outdoor rooftop massage through the hotel's spa.

23. PRIME AT THE BENTLEY HOTEL

For a fantastic eye-to-eye view of the 100+ year-old Queensboro Bridge and one of its two masonry towers, made famous by F. Scott Fitzgerald in The Great Gatsby, Simon and Garfunkel in the 59th Street Bridge Song (Feelin' Groovy), and countless movies, visit Prime at the Bentley, twenty-one floors above the East River on Manhattan's Upper East Side. A large two-story indoor "Penthouse" restaurant, Prime also offers several outdoor tables when the weather is fine, and these are highly recommended. Request one of the five tables on the north-facing terrace for the must-see Queensboro Bridge, Roosevelt Island Aerial Tram and East River views.

When the weather is less cooperative, catch the view through floor-to-ceiling windows inside. Still, make sure to request the tables with the north-east facing views.

This dressy, strictly Kosher restaurant offers steak, fish and sushi, plus a full bar. No bacon on your $27 burger here, although they do offer "facon," a bacon-like facsimile. Come prepared to pay a premium for the unique combination of a 21st-floor New York City rooftop and Kosher food, and then enjoy looking at all 3,724 feet of the magnificent, century-old Queensboro Bridge.

Prime

Location: Upper East Side

Address: 500 E. 62nd St. NY, NY 10065, at York Ave.

Phone: 212.933.9733

bentley.primehospitalityny. com

Subway:

④ ⑤ ⑥

Subway Stop: 59th St.

Calendar: Year-round, outdoor rooftop seating weather permitting

Hours: Sun-Thu 5:30pm-10:30pm, Sat one hour after sundown until late

Reservations: Strongly suggested

$$$$

Photo by Heather Shimmin

24. THE IDES
AT THE WYTHE HOTEL

Magnificent city views that can be seen
only when you are outside Manhattan
are waiting for you from this sprawling,
sparsely furnished sixth floor roof deck.
The Ides Bar is definitely Brooklyn chic
while the crowd takes advantage of the
loose dress code. On any given night,
you might find an assortment of sneaker-
laden tourists, dressed-down hipsters,
dressed-up City types, representatives
of the Bridge and Tunnel crowd, plus a
smattering of Europeans. Taking its cue
from the farm-to-table vibe in Reynard's,
the restaurant downstairs, Ides uses fresh
juices in its cocktails, serves biodynamic
wine, locally distilled spirits and craft beers.
The stylish indoor lounge comes complete
with mosaic tiles, red banquettes and floor-
to-ceiling windows. Spectacular sunsets
and night-time views of everything from
the Williamsburg Bridge to Brooklyn water
towers and even into Queens are what
make The Ides Bar a rooftop destination
not to be missed anytime of year, although
summertime is best.

The Ides

Location: Williamsburg, Brooklyn

Address: 80 Wythe Ave., Brooklyn, NY 11211

Phone: 718.460.8000

wythehotel.com/dining/bar

Subway:

Ⓛ Ⓖ

Subway Stop: L to Bedford Ave. or G to Nassau Ave.

Calendar: Year-round

Hours: Daily 5pm-2am

$$$

Photo courtesy of The Ides Bar

25. BROOKLYN TERRACE AT ALOFT HOTEL

Brooklyn Terrace, the modern indoor-outdoor rooftop lounge, offers views across Brooklyn, over the East River, all the way to the Statue of Liberty. Finding a happy hour on a rooftop can be challenging, but at Brooklyn Terrace, it's easy: Every Tuesday-Friday from 6-8 p.m., this is the place to drop in before a Barclays Center event or when you find yourself in this rapidly gentrifying Brooklyn neighborhood. Regular summer events, when the breezy patio and outdoor seating is at its most irresistible, include Cigar and Wine on Tuesdays and Latin Nights with a live band and plenty of dancing on Fridays. If you can swing an invitation, make sure to RSVP for the Day Parties rooftop brunch for "industry professionals" held on the first and third Saturday and Sunday of the month from 3 until 8 p.m.

Brooklyn Terrace

Location: Downtown Brooklyn

Address: 216 Duffield St. Brooklyn, NY 11201

Phone: 347.390.1891

brooklynterrace.com

Subway:

Ⓐ Ⓒ Ⓕ Ⓡ

Subway Stop: Jay St.-Metrotech

Calendar: Year-round weather permitting

Hours: Tue-Fri 6pm-late, Sat 9pm-late, first and third Sat and Sun "Day Parties" by RSVP from 3pm-8pm

Reservations: Required for some events, otherwise recommended for groups, walk-ins welcome

$$-$$$

Photo by Ari Burling

Upper Elm

Location: North Williamsburg, Brooklyn

Address: 160 N. 12th St. Brooklyn, NY, 11249, between Bedford St. and Berry St.

Phone: 718.218.7500

kingandgrove.com/nyc-hotels/hotel-williamsburg/upper-elm

Subway:

Subway Stop: Bedford St.

Calendar: Year-round

Hours: Wed and Thu 6pm-midnight, Fri and Sat 6pm-2am and Sun 4pm-10pm

$$$

Photo courtesy of Upper Elm

Photo by Heather Shimmin

26. UPPER ELM
AT KING & GROVE
WILLIAMSBURG

Much of the magic of rooftops lies in the change in perspective that being above it all affords, and one of the most magical rooftops is Upper Elm. Just eight stories up and you instantly have wrap-around views of Manhattan's skyline plus sprawling McCarren Park vistas from this super stylish, contemporary rooftop lounge. The signature cocktail list reflects the creative, food-centric North Williamsburg neighborhood, while DJs take advantage of a top-notch sound system. Upper Elm offers many theme events; one not to be missed is Rooftop Reggae on Sundays.

27. Z ROOF
AT Z HOTEL NEW YORK

Drinks, dancing, Skyline Saturday parties and early morning yoga (for hotel guests) make Z Roof a terrific party spot all summer long, with DJs spinning, a full bar and lots of people having a great time. Z Roof's spacious outdoor terrace offers a prime view of the sweeping skyline of New York City. Just outside of Manhattan is a prime place to see the entire sweeping skyline vista, and that is exactly what Z Roof offers on its spacious outdoor terrace. Partiers at Z Roof get a close-up view of the Queensboro Bridge, a view across the East River and a spectacular look at the UN, Citicorp and Chrysler buildings, along with the rest of the mesmerizing lights and familiar shapes of the world's most famous skyline.

While the primary view is across the river, be sure also to check out the view behind the hotel. The well-kept, unmarked building keeping a very low profile is Rolex's American headquarters, and from Z Roof, you can look down onto their magnificent and otherwise completely inaccessible green roof.

Z Hotel provides a free shuttle from 59th and Lexington Avenue in front of H&M every hour on the half hour until 11:30 p.m. However, the last free shuttle back into Manhattan leaves the hotel at 11 p.m. If you miss it, the subway is about a 7-minute walk, or take a quick cab ride across the Queensboro Bridge that you were just admiring from the rooftop.

Z Roof

Location:
Long Island City, Queens

Address:
11-01 43rd Ave. Long Island City, Queens, NY 11101

Phone: 212.319.7000

zhotelny.com/z-roof/

Subway:

Subway Stop:
Court Square and then a 7-minute walk

Best way to get there:
Free shuttle bus from 59th Street and Lexington

Calendar:
Early Jun - mid-Sept

Hours:
Wed, Thu and Sun 6pm-midnight, Fri-Sat 6pm-2am

Reservations:
Depends on the event

$$$

Photo by Ari Burling

Above Rooftop

Location: Staten Island

Address: 1100 South Ave. Staten Island, NY, 10314

Phone: 718.477.2400

aboverooftop.com

Best way to get there: Car

Calendar: Year-round, rooftop terrace open depending on weather

Hours: Thu 5pm-3am, Fri-Sat 9pm-3:30am

Reservations: Required for bottle service

$$$

Photo courtesy of Above Rooftop

28. ABOVE ROOFTOP
AT HILTON GARDEN INN STATEN ISLAND

Ladies, put on your little black dress and high heels. Gents, don your best loafers and button-down shirts. Above Rooftop has arrived and feels more like Vegas, Miami or a swanky Manhattan rooftop lounge than Staten Island. Since Mr. Nicotra bothered to build the only upscale indoor-outdoor hotspot in Staten Island, it seems fair that you dress with care when you visit. In fact, on most nights, you'll see this distinguished looking gentleman in an impeccable suit, crisp shirt and perfectly knotted tie working his way across the busy floor, introducing himself to patrons of his trendy rooftop lounge.

The outdoor rooftop, a beautifully appointed narrow terrace complete with fire pits, is open whenever weather is amenable. From this ninth floor aerie, enjoy the views across the Goethels Bridge into New Jersey. Inside, the open kitchen offers small plates cooked right in front of you.

DJ-spun music throbs throughout the house. With no separate dance floor, dancers claim spots to shake what they've got.

In the middle of the room and on the outdoor terrace are couches and tables reserved for bottle service patrons. The rest of us are welcome to hang out at the very large and spectacularly lit bar or amongst the tables inside or cabanas and fire pits outside. Happy hour is every Thursday from 5-8 p.m. with reduced bottle service prices, and drinks, wine and beer at half price. Every Friday night is "reverse happy hour" all night long, but on Saturday night, bring the Platinum Card. And in this most outer of boroughs, make sure you have a car or two-way cab fare, as you probably don't want to walk the six and half miles from the ferry terminal in your best party shoes.

STK ROOFTOP NYC

Rooftop bars and restaurants not attached to New York City hotels offer a wide array of rooftop experiences. These neighborhood venues frequently attract locals, so if you're looking to share an evening with a rooftop full of real New Yorkers, try the huge variety of elevated food and drink destinations in this section.

Whether you're looking for a wildly romantic rooftop bar in a surprising Manhattan location (Gallow Green), a super casual neighborhood hangout in Brooklyn (The Rock Shop) or a great selection of beers in a Meatpacking District Irish pub (The Brass Monkey), Section 2 will keep your inner roof explorer well fed, watered and entertained.

SECTION 2:
ROOFTOP BARS AND RESTAURANTS

Hotel Chantelle

Location: Lower East Side

Address: 92 Ludlow St. NY, NY 10002, between Broome and Delancey

Phone: 212.254.9100

hotelchantelle.com

Subway:

Subway Stop: F to Delancey St, or J/Z or M to Essex St.

Calendar: Year-round

Hours: Daily 6pm-11pm, Sat and Sun brunch noon-5pm

Reservations: Suggested

$$-$$$

Photo by Ari Burling

29. HOTEL CHANTELLE

To get the full experience of Hotel Chantelle, go there twice: once for the jazz brunch (an exceptionally good value), and again for the wild night life. During brunch on the rooftop, the live music is played quietly enough to allow conversation, the food is consiste[n] pleasing and the 92-cent Bloody Marys are an undeniable deal. T[he] rooftop is retractable, making this a year-round brunch destinatio[n]

but during warm weather under the open sky, this bistro hits its strongest stride.

At night, especially on weekends, Hotel Chantelle, which is not a hotel at all, but a French-Mediterranean restaurant and bar, turns into a three-floor DJ music dance club, with a sweaty basement, a busy ground floor and a hectic rooftop. Bottle service is available, as are specialty cocktails, while the deejays spin definitely danceable sets. Hotel Chantelle is a late-night, weekend destination for trendy 20- or 30-somethings, so arrive early and dress to impress unless you want to wait on line.

30. THE DELANCEY

The Delancey spans three floors, each with a radically different personality. Upstairs from the grungy basement bar is the glamorously sleazy loud downtown music venue, and above that is the Lower East Side version of a lush tropical roof lounge. Not much of a view, but there are plenty of large potted palms, still in their plastic nursery pots, surrounding the inviting red cushion-covered wicker furniture. Loud conversations flow amongst the serious partying, mostly 20-something crowd as there is no music (and no smoking) upstairs. Weekends get very crowded, so show up for happy hour from 5-8 p.m every Monday-Wednesday and from 5-7 p.m. each Thursday. Call The Delancey's friendly staff for information about the occasional late-night happy hour as well. You'll pay a cover charge on Saturday nights in the summer season, but I'd always recommend making a reservation. The retractable roof and heaters make the Delancey's rooftop bar a year-round, subway-close tropical destination.

The Delancey

Location: Lower East Side

Address: 168 Delancey St. NY, NY 10002, at Clinton St.

Phone: 212.254.9920

thedelancey.com

Subway:

Subway Stop: F to Delancey, or J/Z or M to Essex St.

Calendar: Year-round

Hours: Daily 5pm-4am

Reservations: Yes

$$

Photo by Heather Shimmin

31. STK ROOFTOP NYC

STK Rooftop NYC is a super sexy seasonal lounge and restaurant in the heart of the see-and-be-seen Meatpacking District. Seductive ambient music is heard just loud enough to create the vibe but not interfere with private conversations. The long, handsome couches are arranged perfectly for groups having cocktails, or couples wanting to snuggle up with a pitcher of mojitos close by. You'll find plenty of tables in the middle and back of the rooftop if you want to sit down for a meal.

In this converted industrial space, designed to be soothing and relaxing, STK retained the weathered bricks, but added contemporary, comfortable furniture, eye-pleasing greenery, and transparent parapets for maximal viewing of the High Line, the Hudson River and the new downtown Whitney Museum. Oversized market umbrellas protect early arrivals from the heat, but as the sun sets and evening falls, strings of white bulbs light up and STK Rooftop really shines.

STK Rooftop NYC

Location:
Meatpacking District

Address: 26 Little West 12th St. NY, NY 10014, between Washington St. and Ninth Ave.

Phone: 646.624.2441

stkhouse.com

Subway:
Ⓐ Ⓒ Ⓔ Ⓛ

Subway Stop: L to Eighth Ave. or A/C/E to 14th St.

Calendar: Seasonal; usually Apr through mid-Oct

Hours: Sun noon-10pm, Mon- Fri 5pm-midnight, Sat noon-12:30am

Reservations: Suggested

$$$

Photo courtesy of STK Rooftop NYC

75

High Line Food Court

Location: Meatpacking District/Chelsea

Address: Beginning above Tenth Ave. above Little West 12th St. to the area above W. 18th St.

Phone: 212.206.9922

thehighline.org

Subway:

Subway Stop: L to Eighth Ave. or A/C/E to 14th St.

Calendar: Mid-April through late Oct

Hours: Vendors' hours are 11am-9pm daily

$-$$$

Photos by Heather Shimmin

32. HIGH LINE FOOD COURT HIGH LINE PARK

When the High Line opened in June 2009, if visitors wanted something to drink or eat, they usually scurried down the stairs to Chelsea Market, bought their snack or beverage and brought it back up the High Line stairs to enjoy the plantings, public art, various cityscapes and river views.

Fortunately, all that has changed. Visitors to this exceptional elevated park can now buy excellent coffee, a variety of frozen sweets and delectable savories, and even locally sourced beer and wine on the southern section of the High Line. Only socially responsible vendors are considered for this exclusive food court. It spans the areas above Little West 12th Street and W. 18th Street, with most of the vendors located in the covered area known as the "Chelsea Market Passage," above W. 15th and W. 16th Streets. Adjacent to the Chelsea Passage is "The Porch," which seats 40, and is the only area where wine and beer are allowed. Bistro tables and chairs are scattered about the Chelsea Market Passage, in addition to all the benches and lawn seating along the entirety of the park. Open through spring, summer and fall seasons, the carefully curated High Line food vendors offer well-prepared casual meals, snacks and drinks that make it pleasant to stay a little longer on the only American elevated urban park built on an abandoned freight line.

Brass Monkey

Location:
Meatpacking District

Address: 55 Little West
12th St. NY, NY 10014,
between Washington St. and
Tenth Ave.

Phone: 212.675.6686

brassmonkeynyc.com

Subway:

🚇 L A C E

Subway Stop: L to Eighth
Ave. or A/C/E to 14th St.

Calendar: Year-round

Hours: 11am-4am

$$

Photos by Heather Shimmin

33. BRASS MONKEY

When you've tired of velvet ropes, guest lists and $20 cocktails, head to the Brass Monkey. A pub that leans more Irish than English, Brass Monkey is cherished for its neighborhood vibe in spite of being within dart-throwing distance from the Meatpacking District. In 2008, this popular "local" added a second story and a little rooftop beer garden above that. Now expanded to double its original size, the Brass Monkey rooftop offers restrooms and wheelchair access. Beer aficionados can choose from 75 domestic, import and craft brews, plus a good selection of wine and spirits. This low-key rooftop is a casual place to hang out with old friends or make new ones, enjoy some reasonably priced comfort food and drinks, and take in an unobstructed sunset over the Hudson River.

34. LA BIRRERIA AT EATALY

La Birreria, which translates as The Brewery, is appropriately named, as it is the only rooftop brewery in New York City, serving three made-right-there, unfiltered, unpasteurized and naturally carbonated beers.

Mario Batali, the former Iron Chef, has another hit on his hands at this perpetually packed 160-capacity restaurant and bar on the 15th story above the wildly popular all-things-Italian grocery destination, Eataly. The Batali/Bastianich team has put together a casual menu that is so Northern Italian, you'll think you've crossed over the Alps into Bavaria. House-made sausages and cured meats dominate the limited menu, but there are hefty salads and decidedly satisfying mushroom dishes as well.

Getting to La Birreria can be a challenge since the journey begins downstairs in always-crowded Eataly. After you've wended your way past the gelato stand and elbowed through the dairy area, you'll see the line for La Birreria. The downstairs host will show you to the freight elevator that whisks guests up to the 14th floor. Continue your journey down a hall and up more stairs to reach this rooftop destination. Tables are for parties ordering from the menu; otherwise, join the jovial crowd for a roof-brewed or other craft beer at the long bar.

La Birreria

Location:
Flatiron District

Address: 200 Fifth Ave. NY, NY 10010 at 23rd St.

Phone: 212.937.8910

eataly.com/birreria

Subway:

N **R**

Subway Stop: 23rd St.

Calendar: Year-round

Hours: Sun-Wed 11:30am-10pm, Thu-Sun 11:30am-11pm

$$$

Photos courtesy of La Birreria

230 Fifth

Location:
Flatiron District

Address: 230 Fifth Ave. NY, NY 10001, at the corner of 27th St.

Phone: 212.725.4300

230-fifth.com

Subway:

N **R**

Subway Stop: 28th St.

Calendar: Year-round

Hours: Sat-Sun 10am-4am, Mon-Fri 4pm-4am

Reservations: For bottle service or tables with food and beverage minimums; otherwise it's first-come-first-served

$$$

Photos by Heather Shimmin

35. 230 FIFTH

Potted palms, umbrellas and fruity drinks greet you on this 8,000 square foot rooftop, large enough to accommodate 350 guests. You might momentarily wonder if you are still in New York City; that is, until you look up at what is arguably the best view of the Empire State Building around, plus sweeping city vistas that reach to both the Hudson and East Rivers. Popular for its family-friendly rooftop buffet brunch and barbeque on Saturdays from 10 a.m. until 4 p.m., 230 Fifth really shines as a hopping lounge and rooftop bar that stays open until 4 a.m. every night of the week. There is no cover charge and walk-ins are welcome, but if you want to make sure you get a table, bottle service reservations are a good idea. To keep you toasty outside during the winter months, this year-round rooftop bar offers lots of warm boozy drinks (a favorite is the hot chocolate with two types of Godiva chocolate liqueurs), plenty of heat lamps and a rack of cozy red robes in which to snuggle up.

36. GALLOW GREEN
AT THE McKITTRICK HOTEL

Gallow Green is utterly distinct from the other Manhattan roof bars as it was created by a set designer rather than a landscape architect. Ascending the creaky elevator to the fifth floor, then climbing steep stairs to the sixth magically transports you to a rustic, weathered country rail station, so overgrown that it has almost gone to seed but in the most charming way possible. It is staffed with actors still in character, some who serve, and others who entertain with perhaps a fortune telling or another enchanting surprise. It is romantic, whimsical and rustically elegant.

The dramatic setting and name make sense, as Gallow Green is on the roof of the hit, "Sleep No More," an interactive theater experience based loosely on Shakespeare's most superstitious tragedy, Macbeth. In another Scottish reference, the warehouse-turned-theater is called "The McKittrick Hotel," a family name dating back to 1376. The original Gallow Green, from which the bar takes its name, is located south of Glasgow, Scotland and has been notorious since the 1697 stabbing and burning of the "Paisley Witches."

If all that history makes you hungry and thirsty, food is available to enjoy with signature punches served in large copper bowls and Sleep No More-inspired cocktails. The roving entertainers, twinkling lights, cooling breeze and assortment of seating areas–not to mention an abandoned rail car for large groups– make Gallow Green the most unusual rooftop bar in New York City, and is certain to charm your guests.

Gallow Green

Location: Chelsea

Address: 542 W. 27th St. NY, NY 10001 between Tenth and Eleventh Ave.

Phone: 212.564.1662

mckittrickhotel.com/ gallowgreen

Subway:

Subway Stop: 23rd St.

Calendar: Seasonal

Hours: Mon-Wed 4pm-10:30pm, Thu and Sun noon-10:30pm, Fri-Sat noon-12:45am

Reservations: Strongly suggested

$$$

Photos by Heather Shimmin

37. THE EAGLE BAR NYC

From sailors to Stonewall, the history of the Eagle Bar reveals the evolving story of Manhattan's West Side. Back in 1931, the original Eagle Open Kitchen served as a longshoremen's pub on 11th Avenue. After the 1969 Stonewall riots opened the door for gay bars, The Eagle was officially reincarnated as a gay men's leather bar, with black walls and a grungy motorcycle parked inside. This burly men's bar wasn't just for cruising. It sponsored community-based gay sports teams, raised money for a local AIDS clinic at its weekly Tea Dances and created a float for the annual Gay Pride parade. In 1980, the Eagle was featured in an Al Pacino film, "Cruising." By 2000, the AIDS epidemic shuttered dozens of gay bars, and, after 49 years, the Eagle closed its history-laden doors.

In 2001, the phoenix rose from the ashes when a new owner opened another Eagle in what was a 19th century stables, just a few blocks from the original bar. He imported the black walled, dimly lit décor and the thumping music, and even displayed the dilapidated motorcycle from the original Eagle in this much larger space.

The 2,000 square-foot roof deck was opened two years later, and in good weather, this is the place to enjoy a drink, a smoke or do what Pacino did in the movie – cruise for burly he-men.

The Eagle Bar NYC

Location:
Chelsea

Address: 554 W. 28th St. NY, NY 10001, between Tenth and Eleventh Ave.

Phone: 646.473.1866

eaglenyc.com

Subway:

1

Subway Stop: 28th St.

Calendar: Year-round weather permitting

Hours: Mon and Wed-Sat 10pm-4am, Tue 8pm-4am, Sun 4 pm-4am

$$

Photos by Heather Shimmin

38. BEER AUTHORITY

Got some time to kill before your bus leaves? Head to Beer Authority's third-floor rooftop beer garden, adjacent to the Port Authority bus terminal, and you may end up intentionally missing your ride! Casual is key at this three-level beer joint, sporting a somewhat different personality on each floor. While the sprawling second floor has the largest selection of craft brews on tap, the rooftop above is quiet enough to have a conversation with your drinking buddies. Not much of a view, but it's pleasant to sit outdoors under the stars at night or under umbrellas during the day at the conversation-inducing picnic tables and benches.

Before 9 p.m., Beer Authority is kid-friendly. Casual food is available to all, but, no doubt, the extensive beer choices are the main draw, though the rooftop selection is limited. May through October, no happy hour is offered in the rooftop beer garden, but the other half of the year, it's rooftop happy hour all day and all night long. You might just forget why you bought that bus ticket out of town after all!

Beer Authority

Location:
Hell's Kitchen

Address: 300 W. 40th St. NY, NY 10018, between Eighth and Ninth Ave.

Phone: 212.510.8415

beerauthoritynyc.com

Subway:

 A **C** **E**

Subway Stop: 42nd St - Port Authority

Calendar: Year-round

Hours: Mon-Sat 8am-4am, Sun noon-2am

$$

Photos by Heather Shimmin

Bryant Park Grill

Location:
Midtown

Address: 25 W. 40th St., NY, NY 10018, between Fifth and Sixth Ave.

Phone: 212.840.6500

bryantparkgrillnyc.com

Subway:

B D F M

Subway Stop: 42nd St.-Bryant Park

Calendar: Seasonal

Hours: 11:30am-11pm, Sat and Sun brunch 11:30am-3:30pm

$$$

Photo by Heather Shimmin

Photo courtesy of Bryant Park Grill

39. BRYANT PARK GRILL

Located in one of Manhattan's most charming green spaces, and backing up to one of Manhattan's most recognizable landmarks, the Beaux-Arts styled New York Public Library, the rooftop at Bryant Park Grill is an excellent eatery full of sensory delights. Open seasonally, this charming, second floor umbrella-covered restaurant is a wonderful place to sip a cool cocktail on a summer's eve. It's quieter on this rooftop than in much of Midtown, and the well-prepared food smells and tastes delicious. Finally, the view over Bryant Park is beautiful!

Although it may not be obvious, the famous Bryant Park lawn is, in fact, another of New York City's green roofs. Directly underneath this expanse of green is a giant room storing hundreds of thousands of books for the adjacent New York Public Library. However, this underground room was not dug out for book storage. Until 1912, this giant stone-lined hole in the ground served as the main reservoir for the city and the end point of the Old Croton Aqueduct. Using only gravity, this remarkably sophisticated system delivered water to Manhattan residents from 41 miles away.

No reservations are taken for the Bryant Park Grill's rooftop, so leave a little extra time in case there is a wait for a table. Once you are seated, relax and enjoy this delightful—and historical—Midtown getaway.

40. THE ROOF DECK AND CIGAR LOUNGE AT LARRY FLYNT'S HUSTLER CLUB NEW YORK

This pricey "gentlemen's club" features two floors of scantily clad women gyrating on poles, in laps and, for a price, in private rooms, but if you want to smoke a cigar with your Jameson, Mayor Bloomberg insists you head outdoors.

At Hustler Club, that means going up a flight of stairs to the roof deck, a spacious, heated roof terrace supported by exotically lit Doric columns. The Roman theme seems to end there as potted palms and wicker garden furniture, plus a wall-mounted TV, more likely than not broadcasting sports, complete the décor. Bring your own stogie or buy a cigar there, and enjoy the west-facing view across the West Side Highway toward the Hudson River.

Bargain hunters: On the Hustler website, find a coupon for free admission, and if you don't mind getting there before this late-night club heats up, happy hour is Monday through Friday from 6-8 p.m.

The Roof Deck and Cigar Lounge

Location: Hell's Kitchen

Address: 641 W. 51st St. NY, NY 10019, at West St.

Phone: 212.247.2460

hustlerny.com

Subway:

C E

Subway Stop: 50th St.

Calendar: Year-round

Hours: Mon-Fri 6pm-4am, Sat 8pm-4am and Sun 8pm-2am

$$$ with $25 cover

Photo by Heather Shimmin

Location: Midtown East

Address: 1015 Second Ave, NY, NY 10022, between E. 53rd and E. 54th St.

Phone: 212.207.3777

midtown1015.com

Subway:

Subway Stop: 53rd St-Lexington Ave.

Calendar: Year round

Hours: 11am-4am

$$

Photo courtesy of The Terrace, Midtown 1015

41. THE TERRACE, MIDTOWN 1015 AT SUTTON PLACE

This welcoming, unpretentious Midtown East locals spot has three levels with varying vibes. It's a "regular-Joe" noisy sports bar on the ground floor. Up a flight is a private event/lounge/dance space. On the third floor, in the shadow of the famous "Lipstick Building" where Bernie Madoff made off with other people's fortunes, is the casual rooftop bar and restaurant. It still has something of the "regular-guy" sports bar vibe, but it is also a great place to brunch or lunch on a nice summer's day, have dinner, mingle, enjoy the breeze, and of course drink. At the bar seats overlooking Second Avenue, take in this low-rise Manhattan view, or choose the upholstered seating that is a bit more comfortable and lets you focus attention on your mates. During cooler months, the roof deck is covered and heated, but The Terrace at Midtown 1015 is at its most appealing on fine days when the open sky is the only thing over your head.

42. THE HEIGHTS BAR & GRILL

Come for the flavored frozen margaritas, but stay for the open-air rooftop overlooking the Morningside Heights section of Broadway. This Columbia University students' hang is cheap (lunch specials between 11-4 for $6, and two happy hours from 3-7 and 11 p.m. until closing daily) and cheerful, with friendly staff, a juke box and a super casual atmosphere. Until 1996, this space housed Nacho Mama's Burritos, and Tex-Mex dishes are still the vast majority of the menu, along with burgers and wings, although the weekend brunch menu (Saturday and Sunday from 11-4) offers more varied dishes to complement the $3 brunch mimosas, draft beer, Bloody Marys or champagne.

The retractable rooftop makes this a four-season destination, but the combination of a warm summer evening and a frozen $5 mango margarita on the open-air third floor terrace can't be beat.

The Heights Bar & Grill

Location: Morningside Heights

Address: 2867 Broadway. NY, NY 10025, between W. 111th and W. 112th St.

Phone: 212.866.7035

theheightsnyc.com

Subway:

1

Subway Stop: 116th St.

Calendar: Year-round but rooftop is open-air only during summer months

Hours: 11:30am-4am

$$

Photo by Heather Shimmin

Location: Gowanus/Park Slope

Address: 249 Fourth Ave. Brooklyn, NY 11215, between President St and Carroll St.

Phone: 718.230.5740

therockshopny.com

Subway:

R

Subway Stop: Union St.

Calendar: Year-round

Hours: Mon-Fri 5pm-2am, Fri 5pm-4am, Sat 12pm-4am, Sun 12pm-1am

$$

Photo by Heather Shimmin

43. THE ROCK SHOP

Had enough velvet ropes, bouncers and partiers from the suburbs? Then it's time to check out the rooftop at one of Brooklyn's great dive bars, The Rock Shop. This casual two-floor venue feels like visiting a hipster's cool loft apartment. The ground floor has a performance space where local indie-rock bands jam at maximum volume seven nights a week. Upstairs, the games are on TV, people are drinking beer, chatting with the friendly bartenders, shooting pool or throwing darts and eating some pretty terrific pub food.

this rapidly changing neighborhood surrounding Fourth Avenue and Carroll Street, the back of the bar opens to a roof deck large enough for groups of friends to drink, catch up and have a smoke if so inclined. There is plenty of casual seating and a quintessentially New York sliver view across the street of turn of the 19th into 20th century cornices decorating the neighboring 100-year-old rooftops along Fourth Avenue.

big draw is the extended happy hour Monday through Friday from 5 until 8 p.m. Drinks are so discounted on Saturday from noon until 4 p.m. and Sunday nights from 10:30 p.m. until the place closes up at 1 a.m.

44. BERRY PARK BEER GARDEN

There's casual and then there's Brooklyn casual—Berry Park's rooftop beer garden falls into the latter category. Just rolled out of bed? Slip on your flip flops and well-worn t-shirt, and you'll fit right in with the Saturday and Sunday rooftop brunch crowd. Or if you get out of bed much later in the day, as do many Williamsburg and Greenpoint hipsters, head over any summer evening in the same anti-fashion attire. At Berry Park, enjoy the Brooklyn version of a German beer garden with something no place in Europe can offer – stunning views across the East River of the lit-up Manhattan skyline.

The 100-plus seat third-floor rooftop isn't fancy, but with a large selection of mostly German beers on tap--everything from a wheat beer from Germany's oldest brewery to a black lager with subtle malt flavor-- you'll have what you need to wash down the sausage platter and the giant Bavarian pretzels on the menu. And just to remind you you're in Brooklyn rather than Birstein, don't miss the deep-fried house-made pickles.

Berry Park Beer Garden

Location: North Williamsburg/Greenpoint

Address: 4 Berry St. Brooklyn, NY 11211, near N. 14th St.

Phone: 718.782.2829

berryparkbk.com

Subway:

L **G**

Subway Stop: L to Bedford Ave or G to Nassau Ave.

Calendar: Year-round, retractable roof during winter

Hours: Sun-Thu noon-2am, Fri-Sat noon-4am

$$

Photo by Ari Burling

Fornino – The Art & Science of Pizza

Location: Brooklyn Bridge Park

Address: Pier 6, Brooklyn Bridge Park, Brooklyn, NY 11201

Phone: 718.422.1107

forninopizza.com

Subway:

2 **3**

Subway Stop: Clark St.

Best way to get there: Bicycle

Calendar: Seasonal

Hours: Fri 4pm-11pm, Sat-Sun noon-11pm

$$-$$$

Photos by Heather Shimmin

45. FORNINO –
THE ART & SCIENCE OF PIZZA, PIER 6, BROOKLYN BRIDGE PARK

Until 2009, at the bottom of Atlantic Avenue, Pier 6 was an industrial site in a post-industrial location. Now it is a beloved destination in the largest ongoing park project in New York City. Brooklyn Bridge Park will eventually encompass 85 acres, reclaiming the Brooklyn waterfront for 1.3 continuous miles of recreation.

A Williamsburg favorite, Fornino has set up a wood-fired brick pizza oven and a full bar on the roof of Pier 6. Thin-crust pizzas are made with super-fresh local ingredients, several Brooklyn brews are on tap, and the staff is friendly and efficient. The "biergarten" style benches and plastic beer cups keep it casual, but the completely unobstructed views across the East River of lower Manhattan, Governors Island and the Statue of Liberty can't be beat, even at the fanciest locations. The three sand volleyball courts adjacent to Fornino's rooftop give a great excuse to watch the bikini and board shorts-wearing hard bodies work up a sweat as they thump and dig. Open seasonally, and then only Friday through Sunday, it's worth planning your summer weekend dining and sunset-watching around Pier 6's unbeatable rooftop.

Malibu Rooftop Deck

Location: South Bronx inside Yankee Stadium adjacent to Section 310 on the Terrace/Grandstand Level

Address: One 161st St. Bronx, NY 10451

Phone: 718.293.4300

newyork.yankees.mlb.com/nyy/ticketing/spaces_malibu.jsp

Subway:

Subway Stop: 161st St-Yankee Stadium

Calendar: Home games during baseball season

Hours: When the stadium's gates open until end of the seventh inning

$$-$$$

Photos by Heather Shimmin

46. MALIBU ROOFTOP DECK AT YANKEE STADIUM

Fans of the blue and white pinstripes wait for opening day each April when the 27-time World Champion Bronx Bombers return to "The House that Ruth Built" for nine more innings of Americana. The new Yankee Stadium, built in the shadow of the original beloved ball park, offers game attendees willing to spare plenty of cash many swanky upgrades, including a rooftop bar and grill. Naming rights were bought by the famous rum importer, Malibu Rum, so it's no surprise the Malibu Rooftop Deck features high-priced rum specialty drinks, as well as other spirits and a small selection of beers, including two microbrews, one of which is made in New York State. A limited grill menu of hot dogs, sausage, burgers or chicken kebobs holds no culinary surprises, but you didn't come here for the food. What you get with your Yankee Stadium-priced drinks and grub is a large sundeck where you can hang out before or during the game with wide vistas down into Manhattan and up into the South Bronx.

47. PINE BAR & GRILL

Be pleasantly surprised by the smart rooftop space at Pine Bar & Grill in the Southeast Bronx. It is a splash of Manhattan with a dash of South Beach and just a pinch of the Bronx. The modern décor of this surprisingly spacious and inviting rooftop bar includes comfy benches adorned with plush pillows, a smart marble bar and potted palms.

There are no reservations for the rooftop, except for those requesting bottle service, so arrive when it opens, which is as soon as it cools off (times vary between 6-8 p.m.) for a bite to eat and a casual drink. If the roof is open before 7, you can enjoy half-priced drinks in this open-air Bronx oasis. As with many rooftop bars, what starts out as a quiet place to get an al fresco drink transforms into a loud and crowded scene on weekend nights when deejays spin and the partiers arrive.

There is valet parking for drivers, and most of the Pine's patrons drive or work/live close by. While this off-the-beaten-track gem is certainly a worthwhile destination, remember to account for the 10 minute or so hike from the subway in a neighborhood without many yellow cabs.

Pine Bar & Grill

Location: Bronx

Address: 1634 Eastchester Rd. Bronx, NY 10461

Phone: 718.319.0900

pinebargrill.com

Subway:

Subway Stop: Westchester Square-East Tremont Ave.

Calendar: Seasonal

Hours: Opens 6-8pm until 1:45am

$$-$$$

Photos courtesy of Pine Bar & Grill

LAURIE M. TISCH ILLUMINATION LAWN

It is often assumed that a trip to New York City will break the bank, but the elevated parks listed in Section 3 cost little or nothing to visit and offer you million-dollar views and once-in-a-lifetime experiences.

Whether you traverse the length of the High Line on the West Side (free), swim in a Harlem rooftop 50-meter pool ($3) or lounge on a double-decker pier that juts out 500 feet into the East River (free), New York City's elevated parks offer some of the best deals – and views – in town.

SECTION 3:
ELEVATED PARKS

Irish Hunger Memorial

Location: Battery Park City

Address: Vesey St. at North End Ave. NY, NY 10281

Phone: 212.267.9700

batteryparkcity.org/Visit/ Museums-And-Memorials/ Irish-Hunger-Memorial.php

Subway:

2 3 E

Subway Stop: 2/3 to Park Place or E to World Trade Center

Best way to get there: Subway, bicycle

Calendar: Year-round

Hours: Open daily from dawn until dusk

Free

Photo by Ari Burling

48. IRISH HUNGER MEMORIAL

Immerse yourself in a quarter-acre of the Emerald Isle on the sloping green roof that caps the Irish Hunger Memorial, a thought-provoking, multi-sensory homage to "An Gota Mór," Gaelic for "The Great Hunger," widely known as The Great Potato Famine. Between 1845-1852, nearly one million Irish starved to death and nearly another million emigrated to New York City in a desperate attempt to stay alive.

Artist Brian Tolle's edifice leads visitors through a tunnel made of ancient Kilkenny limestone. The tunnel is full of music, spoken word and backlit written texts offering heartbreaking details regarding the historical Irish and current world famines. This passageway opens into an authentic ruined Irish fieldstone cottage donated by the Slack family from County Mayo. Moving forward, visitors climb the gently sloping green roof, one quarter of an acre supported by 230,000 pounds of cantilever re-bar. The plantings, designed by landscape architect Gail Wittwer-Laird, are comprised of 60 varieties of Irish flora. With foxglove, blackthorn, ling heather and indigenous Irish grasses, it feels as if a bit of Ireland has landed on this rooftop in lower Manhattan. Large engraved stones, one from each of Ireland's 32 counties, adorn the green roof that overlooks the Statue of Liberty and Ellis Island, poignant reminders of the refuge sought by The Potato Famine victims.

49. ELEVATED ACRE

Located more than 30 feet above ground lies a wood-planked beach-style boardwalk and nearby dunes bursting with native plants. Though not in plain sight, this exceptional space called the Elevated Acre holds handsome rewards for intrepid explorers.

One of just two elevated "Publically Owned Private Spaces" (POPS) in Manhattan, the Elevated Acre was given new life when it re-opened in 2005 after a three-year, $7 million renovation.

If some of the Acre's elements (the exceptional lighting, use of native plant species and the modern seating) feel vaguely familiar, give yourself a gold star for noticing. Ken Smith Landscape Architect designed this project just a few years before he collaborated on the nearby Pier 15 green roof and East River Esplanade.

Although sandwiched between the 13-story 55 Water Street office building and the 54-story south tower, this above-ground garden and performance art venue affords expansive vistas of the Brooklyn Bridge, the East River, Governor's Island and Pier 6's heliport.

In the middle of the Elevated Acre is an artificial turf-lined amphitheater that is one of the homes of the annual River to River Festival. Free films and a myriad of other cultural events happen here each summer.

While a beautiful garden and view spot by day, the Elevated Acre has a different feel when the sun goes down. At dusk, the focal point becomes the 50-foot, glowing lantern constructed of translucent glass that is built on the northeast corner of the Acre. A mood creator for people on the Elevated Acre, the changing colored lights also act as a beacon for boats floating down the East River as well as for Brooklyn riverfront promenaders.

Elevated Acre

Location: Financial District

Address: 55 Water St. NY, NY 10041 between Old Slip and Broad St.

Subway:

② ③ Ⓡ Ⓙ Ⓩ ④ ⑤

Subway Stop: 2/3 to Wall St. or R to Whitehall St. or J/Z to Broad St. or 4/5 to Bowling Green

Calendar: Year-round

Hours: 8am-9pm

Free

Photo by Ari Burling

111

Location: Financial District, East River Esplanade, just south of South St. Seaport

Address: South St. at Fletcher St.

Subway: 2/3

2 3 4

Subway Stop: Wall St.

Calendar: Year-round

Hours: Lower level 6am-midnight, upper level 8am-dusk

Free

Photo by Ari Burling

50. PIER 15
AT THE EAST RIVER ESPLANADE

Sleek and urban, modern and inviting, with knock-out views in every direction: that's Pier 15. Gorgeous all day, and more beautiful at dusk, this structure's elegance shines through even more brightly when the superbly well-designed lighting scheme comes on.

This pier juts out 500 feet into the East River, affording spectacular views of the Brooklyn Bridge to the north, Brooklyn Heights to the east and directly behind, the collection of high rise buildings that comprise the Financial District. To the south, take in the expanse of the East River and Governors Island. No matter where one looks, it is fabulous NYC-flavored eye candy.

The current highlight of this riverfront ribbon park is the exceptionally well designed, double-decked Pier 15, with gardens and river access below, elevated lawns above, and ample, fun seating everywhere. Double-wide tropical hardwood benches on the lower level encourage people to snuggle up, while Adirondack chairs on the upper deck invite contemplation. Or choose to relax on single lounge chairs, traditional park benches, kidney-shaped seats or amphitheater style steps. Visit the café/bar on the lower level, or bring your own picnic, but either way, grab a fabulous seat and enjoy this fantastic urban rooftop experience.

51. RIVERPARK *(Restaurant and public space)* AT THE ALEXANDRIA CENTER

Leave behind the hustle and bustle of Manhattan for a couple of hours when you dine or picnic on Riverpark's "patio" or "terrace." Crowning a hidden parking structure, these al fresco dining options make delicious use of this rooftop space. The busy FDR roadway lies between you and the East River, but the fantastic water and Brooklyn views are otherwise unobstructed. Maybe because it is hidden in a mostly untraveled part of town, this peaceful destination with farm-to-table fantastic food, attentive service and fresh seasonal cocktails never feels crowded.

While the "patio" is, in fact, an extension of the indoor restaurant, the "terrace" is a public park, open to anyone who chooses to enjoy its park benches and tables. So while the Modern-American cuisine at this excellent Colicchio-owned restaurant is highly recommended, those on a tight budget can take advantage of this unique riverside setting while enjoying a brownbag picnic. Or, for another thrifty option, consider the delicious takeout fare at 'wichcraft, the upscale sandwich shop, also owned by Colicchio, just outside The Alexandria Center building.

For more information on Riverpark's innovative mobile chef's farm, please see Section 5, Listing 78.

Riverpark at the Alexandria Center

Location: Kips Bay

Address: 450 E. 29th St. NY, NY 10016, east of First Ave.

Phone: 212.729.9790

riverparknyc.com

Subway:

6 L

Subway Stop: 6 to 28th St. then long walk, L to 1st Ave. then long walk

Best way to get there: M9 bus or bicycle

Calendar: Year-round

Hours: 6am-1am

Free

Photo by Heather Shimmin

Location: Meatpacking District/Chelsea.

Address: Gansevoort and Washington St. until W. 30th St. between 10th and 11th Ave.

Phone: 212.500.6035

thehighline.org

Subway:

Subway Stop: A/C to 14th St. or L to Eighth Ave. or C/E to 23rd St.

Calendar: Year round

Hours: Dec-Mar 7am-7pm, Apr-May and Oct-Nov 7am-10pm, Jun-Sept 7am-11pm

Free

Photo of the Standard Hotel from the Highline by Ari Burling

52. THE HIGH LINE

The elevated sliver of earthly paradise called The High Line opened in 2009. In 2011, it was expanded to a mile in length, wending through the Meatpacking District and Chelsea. The final section, another half mile of heaven called High Line at the Rail Yards, will be opened in three phases beginning in 2014.

With the rise of interstate trucking in the 1950s, the southern section of the High Line's original 13 miles of trestles was no longer deemed necessary, and was demolished in 1960. The last train rumbled down what was left of its tracks in 1980. After that, the sections above the Hudson Rail Yards at W. 34th Street were dismantled. What remained lay unused and was considered by many to be an eyesore and crime magnet.

In 1999, two neighbors had the vision to metamorphose this abandoned rail line into an elevated park. They created Friends of the High Line, and thus began the amazing story that has transformed the far West Side from an area of Manhattan to be avoided into the destination not to be missed. In 2012 alone, about four and a half million visitors traversed this elevated park 30 feet above the ground to enjoy its extraordinary plantings, myriad of cultural events, enticing eating and relaxing options, and elevated perspective of the surrounding urban landscape.

53. ROBERT MOSES PLAZA
AT FORDHAM UNIVERSITY
LINCOLN CENTER CAMPUS

Hidden in plain sight, this massive roof garden is a remarkably well-kept secret considering that tens of thousands of people walk or ride past it each day completely unaware of its existence. At the top of an unassuming, tucked-away staircase near W. 60th Street and Columbus Avenue lies a massive rooftop garden with mature trees, spacious lawns, a vine-covered arbor and a delightful sculpture garden. High rise buildings surround this plaza with a small slice of the Hudson River on view from the west end of the garden.

On top of the Quinn Library at Fordham University's Manhattan Campus rests this rooftop oasis. It is named after the former Parks commissioner who secured the real estate for a massive redevelopment project that included the creation of Lincoln Center and the expansion of Fordham University out of the Bronx and into Manhattan. This roof garden, dedicated in 1970, with remarks made personally by Robert Moses, serves as the central plaza for the Manhattan campus.

Even on the warmest summer days, a cooling breeze off the Hudson River can be felt on the lawn under one of the many large trees. Though it is well used by students and faculty at this private Jesuit university, the Robert Moses Plaza maintains a serene, quiet vibe. When looking for a nearby getaway from the hectic streets of the Upper West Side, consider making an easy escape to this often overlooked rooftop park.

Robert Moses Plaza

Location: Lincoln Center/ Upper West Side

Address: W. 61st St. and Columbus Ave. NY, NY 10023, take the stairs or elevator to enter the plaza and sculpture garden

Phone: 212.636.6000

fordham.edu

Subway:

Subway Stop: 59th St.- Columbus Circle

Calendar: Year-round

Hours: Dawn-dusk

Free

Photo by Heather Shimmin

119

Laurie M. Tisch Illumination Lawn

Location: Lincoln Center (Northwest Section)

Address: Overlooking W. 65th St. between Broadway and Amsterdam Ave.

lc.lincolncenter.org

Subway:

Subway Stop: 66th St-Lincoln Center

Calendar: Year-round except during lawn rejuvenation

Free

Photo by Ari Burling

54. LAURIE M. TISCH ILLUMINATION LAWN

One of only a handful of public-access roof lawns in Manhattan, the gently sloping turf of the Illumination Lawn, even on the hottest days, is the perfect place to enjoy a breeze and take a load off your Upper West Side-weary feet. Muse over the Henry Moore sculpture, "Reclining Figure," in the adjacent reflecting pool, take a picnic, or take a nap, but make sure to enjoy this Manhattan lawn in the sky.

A green roof in the highly original shape of a large warping parabola caps the lauded Lincoln Ristorante and the Elinor Bunin Munroe Film Center in the northwest section of the Lincoln Center campus. The pointed exterior of the recently renovated Alice Tully Hall across W. 65th Street echoes the point of this rooftop parabola. Designed by the same team who created the High Line, Diller Scofidio + Renfro, the 7,200 square foot Illumination Lawn has easy access via built-in steps at its base, so climbing onto this roof is perfectly safe.

Hidden green roofs abound at Lincoln Center, so when enjoying the Illumination Lawn, take a moment to notice two less obvious ones. The adjacent Barclay Capital Grove was planted using green roof technology, similar to that at the National September 11 Memorial, and the Claire Tow Theater, a 112-seat experimental playhouse built on top of the Beaumont, sports a green roof surrounding its outdoor deck.

Location: Midtown

Address: 725 Fifth Ave. NY, NY 10022, at 56th St.

trump.com/Real_Estate_ Portfolio/New_York/Trump_ Tower/Trump_Tower.asp

Subway:

N R Q

Subway Stop: Fifth Ave-59th St.

Calendar: Year-round

Hours: Open during store hours

Free

Photos by Heather Shimmin

55. TRUMP TOWER

Weary Fifth Avenue shoppers, read this! Two roof gardens are waiting plus indoor space and restrooms for you to take a load off your feet. These unique spaces offer everyone what only the super-rich can have: A great vantage across W. 56th and W. 57th Streets toward some of the most coveted shopping venues on Fifth Avenue.

One of only two elevated "Publically Owned Private Spaces" (POPS) in Manhattan (the other is the Elevated Acre at 55 Water Street), Trump Tower was built by Donald Trump in 1983, with two publically accessible roof terraces, one south-facing on the fourth floor, and the other north-facing on the fifth floor. Combined, these seemingly forgotten roof terraces total over 6,300 square feet.

Signage leading to these public spaces is minimal, so follow my directions to find these tucked away spaces: Head indoors to the shopping atrium, past the many marble, glass, brass and mirrored surfaces. Go up the escalators in front of the waterfall to the fourth floor. On your right, you'll find a glass door to the smaller of the two rectangular roof terraces. If you are looking for the larger outdoor space, return to the escalator and ascend one additional floor. Turn left to find the glass door.

This larger terrace seems to have been originally designed as a beautiful public space, although the maintenance schedule appears to be a bit lax. Regardless, these two hidden roof terraces offer a quiet refuge in which to relax and rejuvenate before the shopping spree continues.

56. RIVERBANK STATE PARK

When New York City desperately needed a new sewage treatment plant, and urban planners determined it should be built in Harlem along the banks of the Hudson River, local residents were mighty perturbed. The city sweetened the deal by promising local residents an enormous new park bursting with recreational facilities on top of the plant. And that is how, in 1993, the only 28-acre rooftop park in the Western hemisphere came into existence in Northern Manhattan.

Five major buildings are dotted throughout the park: an indoor Olympic-size pool, a covered skating rink that offers ice skating during the winter and roller skating the rest of the year, an 800-seat theater, a 2,500-seat athletic complex with a fitness room and a 150-seat restaurant.

But with 28 acres of rooftop at play, there is room for much more: a 25-yard lap pool and wading pool open from July 4th through Labor Day, four tennis courts, four basketball courts, a lighted softball field, four handball courts, a 400-meter eight-lane running track built around a field appropriate for football or soccer, two playgrounds, a water-splashing area, several picnic areas and a summertime carousel. There is even a rooftop community garden at Riverbank!

Scores of rooftop classes are offered for all age groups, including just about everything from belly dancing and salsa lessons to chess instruction, painting classes to tennis coaching, and playing guitar to practicing Tai Chi. Early morning swimmers watch the pink and orange sky turn blue over the river as they walk across the rooftop park toward the pool complex, the only place in Manhattan one can swim in a well-maintained 50-meter pool for a mere $3 entry fee.

Being 69 feet above and alongside the Hudson River affords Riverbank Park visitors additional advantages. There are unfettered views across the Hudson of the pristine New Jersey Palisades and the river-spanning George Washington Bridge. For more than 20 years, Harlem residents have stayed fit at this enormous rooftop wonder.

Riverbank State Park

Location: Harlem

Address: : 679 Riverside Dr. NY, NY 10031; entrances at W. 138th St. and W. 145th St.

Phone: 212.694.3600

nysparks.com/parks/93/details.aspx

Subway:

Subway Stop: 137th St. or 145th St.

Calendar: Year-round

Hours: 6am-11pm but some of the facilities within the park are open seasonally or with limited hours (skate rink, pools, carousel, etc.)

Free-$

Photos by Heather Shimmin and Arlene Bender

GARDEN OF STONES AT
THE MUSEUM OF JEWISH HERITAGE

Rooftops in Section 4 span all five of New York City's distinct boroughs. Rooftops everywhere, from the top of the Bronx to the bottom of Staten Island, into Queens and Brooklyn and throughout Manhattan, make Section 4 perfect for the most intrepid of roof explorers.

Visit New York City's oldest green roofs atop Fort Tompkins and Battery Weed that offer glorious views from under the Verrazano Narrows Bridge. Pay homage at one of the City's newest green roofs at the National September 11 Memorial. And learn about some of the most up-to-date green building techniques, while enjoying the unique beauty of the leaf-shaped green roof at the Brooklyn Botanic Gardens Visitors Center.

SECTION 4:
MUSEUMS, THEATERS AND GREEN ROOFS

57. THE NATIONAL SEPTEMBER 11 MEMORIAL

One of Manhattan's most unusual green roofs does not appear to be a roof at all. The 9/11 Memorial welcomed over one million visitors in its first three months, and continues to draw enormous crowds daily.

Also known as The National September 11 Memorial, this sprawling plaza is, in fact, an eight-acre green roof, built as much as 70 feet above the 9/11 Memorial Museum, a train station and other below-ground facilities. This "stealth" green roof is home to over 400 swamp white oak trees, all of which are planted in computer-monitored containers to ensure their vitality. One of the many eco-friendly design details built into this high-tech rooftop is that rain water is collected in storage tanks under the pavement. The harvested rain water is later used to irrigate the grove of magnificent oaks that can potentially reach 60 feet in height.

In the midst of the rooftop oak grove is the centerpiece of the 9/11 Memorial. The two spectacular waterfalls, each one acre in size, were built inside the footprints of the original Twin Towers and are surrounded by the names of the 2,753 victims who lost their lives in the devastating 2001 terror attack.

The National September 11 Memorial

Location: Battery Park City

Address: Liberty Street, NY, NY 10006. Entrance at the northwest corner of Albany and Greenwich St.

Phone: 212.266.5211

911memorial.org

Subway:

Ⓐ Ⓒ Ⓙ Ⓩ ② ③ ④ ⑤

Subway Stop: Fulton St.

Calendar: Year-round

Hours: Mar-Sept 10am-8pm, Oct-Feb 10am-6pm

Reservations: Strongly recommended

Free

Photo by Ari Burling

Garden of Stones

Location: Battery Park City

Address: 336 Battery Place. NY, NY 10280

Phone: 646.437.4202

mjhnyc.org

Subway:

Subway Stop: Bowling Green

Calendar: Year-round

Hours: Sun-Tue and Thu 10am-5:45pm, Wed 10am-8pm, Nov-Mar Fri 10am-3pm; Apr-Oct Fri 10am-5pm

$ (Free Wednesdays 4-8pm)

Photos by Heather Shimmin

58. GARDEN OF STONES AT THE MUSEUM OF JEWISH HERITAGE

This exceptional 4,150 square foot rooftop garden, overflowing with symbolism and beauty, was created by the celebrated artist Andy Goldsworthy. "Garden of Stones" was commissioned by the Museum of Jewish Heritage as a "contemplative space dedicated to the memory of those who perished in the Holocaust and a tribute to those who survived." It is no accident that this rooftop, memorializing those who lost so much, has an uninterrupted view from Battery Park City across the water to the Statue of Liberty.

In 2003, by the artist's design, each of the specially chosen and prepared 18 hollowed out boulders was planted with a single dwarf oak sapling. Over time, the trees will continue to grow inside the three- to thirteen-ton boulders, roots fusing to the stone, combining the strongest and most fragile of natural elements.

Goldsworthy's works, including this, his only permanent New York City installation, explore the effect of time on humans and nature. In order to document change in the "Garden of Stones," a time-lapse camera is installed above the garden. "Timekeeper" compiles these photos and allows museum visitors to scroll through images of the garden at its inception, when being planted, through the leafy and bare seasons, right up until the most recent picture of this rooftop, taken, at most, two minutes before.

59. THE LOWER EAST SIDE (LES) ECOLOGY CENTER

The Lower East Side Ecology Center is a nonprofit organization dedicated to recycling, composting, sustainability education and stewardship of green spaces in New York City. It seems only fitting that they would install an eco-friendly green roof above their offices.

This 1941 structure had served as a New York City Fire Department Fireboat House for more than 50 years when the Parks Department took over the building. The LES Ecology Center will inherit full use of the building from the Parks employees at the completion of the surrounding East River Park's renovation.

This spot has been part of the Manhattan story for centuries; in fact, its multiple layers of history predate the Dutch settlers. The Lenape Native Americans used to land their canoes at this crucial bend in the fast-flowing East River. The Dutch unloaded provisions from boats here, and this very spot played a strategic role protecting George Washington's troops in the Battle of Brooklyn. In more modern times, fireboats were moored here as early as 1877.

In its latest incarnation as the LES Ecology Center, just south of the Williamsburg Bridge, the green roof offers unobstructed views in all directions. In fact, visitors can look across the East River toward two more public access rooftops – The Brooklyn Grange farm at the Brooklyn Navy Yard and its neighbor, the Ted and Honey Café in Building 92 that offers the option of outdoor dining on their green-roof terrace.

Lower East Side (LES) Ecology Center

Location: Lower East Side

Address: Bottom of Grand St. in the East River Park, NY, NY 10001, east of the FDR Dr, along the water's edge

Phone: 212.477.4022

lesecologycenter.org

Subway:

Ⓑ Ⓓ Ⓕ

Subway Stop: B/D to Grand St. or F to East Broadway (then a 15-20 minute walk)

Best way to get there: Bicycle or the M21 bus

Calendar: Year-round

Hours: Business hours

Free

Photo by Ari Burling

60. SKY ROOM AT THE NEW MUSEUM

Most of the time, the Sky Room is a stunning 2,000 square foot private event space. The eleven-foot ceilings and two all-glass walls lead to an L-shaped terrace 175 feet above the once-seedy Bowery. But each Saturday and Sunday, the seventh floor venue is open to museum goers. Usually 175 feet would represent a height closer to 17 floors, but the New Museum galleries, designed to look like a series of off-kilter boxes, have enormously high ceilings to ensure room for outsized contemporary art installations.

The outdoor terrace at the Sky Room is also a portal through which to view lower Manhattan's history. Over 300 years ago, the land on which the New Museum sits was farmed by Peter Stuyvesant. He was the Director-General of New Netherland (what New York was called before British rule), and this was his "bouwerij," the old Dutch word for farm.

By the 20th century, the Bowery became New York's skid row, an unsavory area with dive bars and flop houses. A living remnant of the skid row era is the New Museum's neighbor, The Bowery Mission, a landmark that has helped countless homeless men for well over 100 years. The south facing terrace of the Sky Room overlooks The Mission's rooftop farm. With gentrification of the Bowery nearly erasing its sketchy past, the Bowery Mission remains a significant historical and social institution. This remarkable rooftop farm is used to grow food for and bring self-respect to the indigent population it serves.

The transformation from sketchy to a safe, trendy neighborhood is nearly complete. The Bowery is currently home to gourmet restaurants, high fashion and stylish hotels, alongside contemporary art galleries and, of course, the biggest galleries of them all at the New Museum.

Sky Room

Location: Bowery

Address: 235 Bowery. NY, NY 10002, near Prince St.

Phone: 212.219.1222

newmuseum.org

Subway:

Subway Stop: Second Ave.

Calendar: Year-round

Hours: Weekends only 11am-6pm

$$

Photo courtesy of
The New Museum

Address: Hudson River Park at W. 22nd St. NY, NY 10011

Phone: 212.767.0470

pier62carousel.com

Subway:

Subway Stop: 23rd St.

Calendar: Open during spring, summer and early fall, weather permitting

Hours: 11am-7pm

$

Photo by Heather Shimmin

61. PIER 62 CAROUSEL AT HUDSON RIVER PARK

At first glance, the 36-foot carousel looks charmingly traditional, but a closer look reveals details that make it the only one of its kind.

Housed under a protective living roof sits the Pier 62 Carousel. Visible only from the north and the east, the green roof does more than protect riders and their wooden carousel critters from the sun. This shed-like cap is topped with just a couple of inches of soil in which tiny tough little plants called sedum grow. There is no irrigation up there; these hardy plants survive by absorbing rain water. The rooftop solar panels collect energy and, on bright days, help to run the carousel mechanism, its energy efficient LED lights and sound system. Finally, the structure holding up the green roof is composed of five trusses that have been repurposed from the truss material in the original pier warehouses.

Most of the 33 hand-carved wood figures are species indigenous to the Hudson River Valley: Choose from a peregrine falcon, green turtle, black bear cub or horseshoe crab. The traditional carousel façade has been left off so riders can see the mechanics of how it all works as the Hudson River view comes around with each rotation of this eco-conscious carousel.

The Lower East Side Girls Club

Location: Lower East Side

Address: 101 Ave. D. NY, NY 10009, between 7th and 8th St.

Phone: 212.982.1633

girlsclub.org

Subway:

Subway Stop: Second Ave. with a 15-20 minute walk

Best way to get there: M8 bus or bicycle

Calendar: Year-round

Hours: Varies

Access: Girls Club members, their families and volunteers

Free

Photo by Heather Shimmin

62. THE LOWER EAST SIDE GIRLS CLUB

In the "bad old days" of crime-ridden 1970s New York City, the Lower East Side, an area especially hard hit in those terrible economic times, lost all of its after-school facilities except one: the Boys Club. In response to this, The Lower East Side Girls Club was eventually established in the 1990s to provide creative and free extracurricular activities for neighborhood girls ages 8-18. In 2013, the LES Girls Club entered a grand new era when it opened its doors to a 30,000 square foot, state-of-the-art, sustainably built facility.

One of the many "centers" in the facility is focused on exposing young women to the environmental sciences. Through the third-floor doors of the "Science and Environmental Education Center" is an accessible green roof where the girls can grow herbs and flowers for the café downstairs, and have a hands-on place to learn about environmental sustainability practices.

63. SHAKE SHACK
IN MADISON SQUARE PARK

All this roof exploring can make you hungry, so be sure to stop by Shake Shack in Madison Square Park to check out the sloping green roof on this beloved burger stand, and while you're there, grab some top-of-the-line comfort food, local beer or organic wine.

Started in 2001 as an all-natural hot dog cart in Madison Square Park, Shake Shack has become the destination for burgers, dogs, frozen creamy treats and more. Graduating from cart to permanent venue, Shake Shack was granted the right to build this burger stand in the northeast corner of the park in 2004, and it seems that there has been a long line of hungry customers ever since. The Madison Square Park Conservancy allowed Shake Shack to be built with the caveat that it fit into the park's natural surroundings; the eye-catching sloping green roof beautifully achieves that goal.

Shake Shack

Location: Flatiron District

Address: SE corner of Madison Square Park near Madison Ave. and E. 23rd St.

Phone: 212.889.6600

shakeshack.com/location/madison-square-park/

Subway:

N R

Subway Stop: 23rd St.

Calendar: Year-round

Hours: 11am–11pm

$$

Photo by Heather Shimmin

64. CLAIRE TOW THEATER AT LINCOLN CENTER

Artfully concealed on the Vivian Beaumont Theater rooftop, the $42 million Claire Tow Theater seems almost hidden in plain sight. Easier to notice from the plaza below when the theater is attractively lit up at night, this modern jewel box, with its $20 per ticket mandate, was built to encourage the next generation of playwrights, directors and designers, as well as audience members. An intimate, 112-seat black box theater is the centerpiece of this 23,000 square foot rooftop complex that also houses rehearsal and office space. For the enjoyment of ticketholders, there is an appealing bar offering casual food, soft drinks, beer and cocktails that can be taken outside to the sizable deck built a few feet above the green roof. From the deck, enjoy the view over the Henry Moore sculpture and the sloping rooftop lawn on the Lincoln Restaurant, and into Avery Fisher Hall, home of the New York Philharmonic.

The only way up to the deck and green roof is a brief ride in one of the two elevators located in the lobby of the Beaumont Theater. These elevators, built between book stacks from the neighboring New York Public Library for the Performing Arts, are available only to ticketholders one hour prior to curtain, and it is well worth it to show up early. The deck, green roof and bar are also open one hour after curtain, so be sure to take advantage!

Claire Tow Theater

Location: Lincoln Center

Address: 150 W. 65th St. NY, NY 10023, between Broadway and Amsterdam Ave.

Phone: 212.239.6200

lct.org/aboutClaireTow.htm

Subway:

Subway Stop: 66th St.

Calendar: Open only when a production is running

Hours: One hour before and after a production

Reservations: Theater ticket is required

$$

Photos by Heather Shimmin

65. THE ARSENAL AT CENTRAL PARK

Built over 160 years ago in 1851, the Arsenal, resembling a medieval castle with its crenelated cornice, was designed as a storage depot for arms and munitions when E. 64th Street and Fifth Avenue was in the middle of virgin land. Central Park, not even a thought until six years later, was completed post-Civil War in 1873, after the Arsenal had stood its ground for more than 20 years.

By then, the Arsenal was no longer serving as a munitions storehouse. Over time, it has played many roles: It was a police station, the original home of the American Museum of Natural History (dinosaur fossils were reconstructed in a studio at the Arsenal), and even a makeshift zoo. During the reign of Robert Moses, the Arsenal became the command post for the Parks Commissioner and so it remains today.

The easily accessible Arsenal rooftop has a storied history of its own. For nearly 50 years, from 1869 through 1918, the Municipal Weather Bureau's instruments were installed on the rooftop of the Arsenal, gathering weather data for New York City.

Where once they served to collect meteorological data, today the three rooftop gardens atop the Arsenal collect a different type of scientific information. The myriad of plant varieties are grown in artfully arranged containers filled with manufactured lightweight soil used to lighten the load that the roof has to carry. This garden demonstrates that bushes, vines, and even trees of some size can be grown successfully in lightweight soil. On the uppermost roof elevation, delicious vegetables and berries are grown in the same man-made medium.

To reach these rooftop gardens, take the stairs or elevator to the fourth floor, and walk (quietly, please) through the Parks Department offices. The doors leading to the two separate roof gardens are on opposite sides of the offices.

The Arsenal

Location: Upper East Side

Address: In Central Park at E. 64th St. NY, NY 10065, just off Fifth Ave.

Phone: 212.360.8163

centralpark.com/guide/attractions/arsenal

Subway:

N Q R

Subway Stop: Fifth Ave-59th St.

Calendar: Year-round

Hours: Mon-Fri 9am-5pm

Free

Photo by Heather Shimmin

143

Location: 1000 Fifth Ave.
NY, NY 10028, at E. 82nd
St.

Phone: 212.535.7710

metmuseum.org

Subway:

Subway Stop: 86th St.

Calendar: Early May-early
Nov, closed during inclement
weather and major holidays

Hours: 10am-5:30pm

$-$$

Photos by Heather Shimmin

66. THE IRIS AND B. GERALD CANTOR ROOF GARDEN AT THE METROPOLITAN MUSEUM OF ART

Each May since 1998, New Yorkers eagerly await the reopening of the 8,000 square foot Cantor Roof Garden, an expansive terrace and exhibit space atop the Metropolitan Museum of Art.

This rooftop offers knock-out views over the green canopy of Central Park, south toward midtown, across to Central Park West and behind for a glimpse of the Upper East Side. In a lucky year, the fiery orange, yellow and red fall foliage begins before the early November closing of this roof. During one of those years, this view is a must-see.

Since the late 1990s, the Cantor Roof Garden has hosted an annual single-artist installation. Roy Lichtenstein, Jeff Koons, Andy Goldsworthy and Roxy Paine are some of its past exhibitors. In 2011 and 2012, the exhibits, Big Bambú (Doug + Mike Starn) and Cloud City (Tomás Saraceno), offered guests the chance to walk through the elevated exhibits, making the view even more expansive and irresistible.

The Cantor Roof Garden is available via only one bank of elevators so first-time guests may have to ask how to get to the rooftop, but be assured it is worth the search. Once you have found the way, take your time to have a drink or a snack, enjoy the outstanding view, the mind-expanding art and the endless people watching. Just don't be in a hurry. Wear a hat as shade can be scarce.

67. THE VERTICAL TOUR AT THE CATHEDRAL CHURCH OF ST. JOHN THE DIVINE

Picture the space in a house above the ceiling and below the roof called an attic or a garret. Imagine that this ceiling is 124 feet from the floor and built of what looks like carved stone with ribbed vaulting. The roof is 168 feet from the floor, making the attic 44 feet in height. Clearly, this isn't just any house; it's a house of worship, and in this particular case, it is the largest Gothic cathedral in the world, and the world's fourth largest church.*

St. John the Divine was conceived of in 1828, construction began in 1892, and to this day is not yet completed. The back of the church is built in the Byzantine/Romanesque style and the front is clearly Gothic, with "height and light" as the predominant features.

Three times a week, the "Vertical Tour" is offered. Not only do visitors traverse the Triforium (the Bishop's Walk), the guide takes the group higher and outside on the roof of one of the flying buttresses that supports this massive structure. Ascending further, above the ceiling and below the roof, guests visit the attic, or "la-Forêt," and see how it's all put together. In most churches, the enormous beams that hold up the roof are made of timber, hence the name "The Forest." At St. John the Divine, la-Forêt is made of steel beams per city building codes. It is dusty and ill-lit but amazing to see the tops of the vaulted cathedral ceiling below you, looking eerily like a series of clay firing kilns, with exposed bricks in symmetrical convex shapes. This unique tour ends under the roof rather than on top of it, and is a must-see for intrepid roof explorers.

*The world's other three largest churches are St. Peter's Basilica at the Vatican, Our Lady of Aparecida in Brazil and the Seville Cathedral in Spain.

The Vertical Tour at The Cathedral Church of St. John the Divine

Location: Upper West Side/ Morningside Park

Address: 1047 Amsterdam Ave. NY, NY 10025, at W. 112th St.

Phone: 212.932.7347

stjohndivine.org

Subway:

Subway Stop: 110th St/ Cathedral Parkway

Calendar: Every Wed and Sat year-round

Hours: Wed at noon and Sat at noon and 2pm

Reservations: Yes (participants must be at least 12 years of age)

$

Photos by Ari Burling

Brooklyn Botanic Garden Visitor Center

Location: Prospect Park, Brooklyn

Address: 900 Washington Ave. Brooklyn, NY 11225

Phone: 718.623.7200

bbg.org

Subway:

2 3 4 5 B

Subway Stop: 2/3/ and 4/5 to Franklin Ave. or B to Prospect Park

Calendar: Year-round

Hours: Mar-Oct: Tue-Fri 8am-6pm, Sat-Sun 10am-6pm, Nov-Feb: Tue-Fri 8am-4:30pm, Sat-Sun 10am-4:30pm

$ (free on Tuesdays and winter weekdays)

Photo by Ari Burling

68. BROOKLYN BOTANIC GARDEN VISITOR CENTER

This outstanding example of a living roof and what it can do for the environment opened at the Brooklyn Botanic Garden as the institution passed its 100-year mark. It is the showpiece in the Garden's "Campaign for the Next Century."

The 9,400 square foot, curvilinear roof meadow atop the new Visitor Center is a complex canvas planted with 40,000 native flowering plants, bulbs and grasses designed to display seasonal changes in color and texture. It's no surprise that the BBG Visitor Center won a New York City Design Commission Award for Design Excellence. The semi-intensive (meaning the plants are in 8 inches of soil) green roof's runoff flows into a daisy-chain series of rain gardens that conserve 200,000 gallons of water annually. The living roof insulates the Visitor Center below it, and reduces storm water overflow by acting like a giant sponge. Designed to attract hummingbirds, butterflies and lots of bees, this living roof has also hosted some surprise visitors. Camouflaged in the roof's tall grasses, a gardener reportedly found a hidden duck nest with six eggs. Human visitors get their best view of this ever-changing eco-forward living roof by walking up to the Overlook amongst the collection of mature gingko trees and enjoying the view from the benches.

69. FACILITIES BUILDING AT BUSHWICK INLET PARK

New York City is reclaiming its waterfront, and Bushwick Inlet Park is a prime example. This previously industrial shoreline strip was rezoned in 2005, and in 2013, Bushwick Inlet Park opened its award winning (Honor Award from the NY Chapter of the American Society of Landscape Architects, among others), sloping, green-roofed facilities building. Employing the entire array of environmentally progressive technologies, this building has geothermal wells for efficient heating-cooling, a system to collect rainwater that is later used for irrigating the green roof, a solar canopy that provides more than 50% of the building's energy needs, and, of course, the green roof to absorb storm water runoff, a pesky New York City infrastructure conundrum. The facilities building is also a public recreation space that provides a shaded, sunny or starlit uninterrupted "hilltop" view of the East River and the Manhattan Skyline. Plus it is a short walk from two terrific North Williamsburg rooftop bars, The Ides Bar at the Wythe Hotel, and Upper Elm at King & Grove.

Facilities Building

Location: North Williamsburg, Brooklyn

Address: Kent Ave. between N. 9th St and N. 12th St.

nycgovparks.org/parks/bushwickinletpark/

Subway:

Subway Stop: Bedford St.

Calendar: Year-round

Free

Photos by Heather Shimmin

151

70. ATLANTIC TERMINAL SUBWAY ENTRANCE AT BARCLAYS CENTER

Since the Brooklyn Dodgers left Ebbets Field in 1957, no professional sports teams have called Brooklyn home. That is, until 2012, when the Brooklyn Nets (basketball) and the New York Islanders (hockey) began playing at the Barclays Center. This center could not have been built without collaboration between public transportation and private development.

In concert with the opening of the $1 billion Barclays Center, a $76 million subway station with 9 subway lines and 11 bus lines plus Long Island Railroad access was put into service. Crowning the 26-foot wide stairwell, designed to get people in and out of the arena quickly, is a sedum-planted green roof. Sloping to as much as 85 degrees, a soil retention system had to be designed to keep the plants anchored in place.

Constructed at one of the busiest urban intersections in New York City, this subway station's green roof is the eco-friendly centerpiece of a vast public plaza that serves as the grand entryway to the long-awaited home of Brooklyn's professional sports teams.

Atlantic Terminal Subway Entrance

Location: Prospect Heights, Brooklyn

Address: 620 Atlantic Ave. Brooklyn, NY 11217, Atlantic and Flatbush Ave.

mta.info

Subway:

Subway Stop: Atlantic Ave-Barclays Center

Calendar: Year-round

Free

Photo by Heather Shimmin

153

Location: Brooklyn Bridge
Park

Address: Piers 1, 5 and
6, Brooklyn Bridge Park,
Brooklyn, NY 11201

Phone: 718.222.9939

brooklynbridgepark.org

Subway:

2 3

Subway Stop: Clark St.

Best way to get there:
Bicycle

Calendar: Seasonal

Hours: Sat-Sun 11am-10pm
weather permitting

$-$$

Photo by Heather Shimmin

71. PIER 5 AMPLE HILLS CREAMERY AT BROOKLYN BRIDGE PARK

A stroll through Brooklyn Bridge Park to see the three green roofs,
starting from the Pier 1 Gatehouse, close to the Brooklyn Bridge,
past the Ample Hills Creamery ice cream stand at Pier 5, and
down to the Pier 6 Gatehouse is a little less than a mile and well
worth the effort. Just as you begin to think about something to cool
you off near the end of this walk, under the second of the triad of
green roofs is an extraordinary ice-cream concession that uses all
natural and completely delicious ingredients. Indulge yourself!

These living roofs host a unique array of plants with overflowing shrubs and flowers chosen for their ability to handle the dry and windy waterside rooftop conditions. Since all three green roofs top one-story buildings, they are easily visible from the ground level of this remarkable park. The roofs insulate the buildings, keeping them warmer in the winter and cooler in the summer. They absorb rain, thereby reducing storm water runoff. They create additional wildlife habitat and lend a helping hand toward reducing heat island effect; as the rooftop rain evaporates it naturally cools the surrounding air.

The Brooklyn Bridge Park Conservancy has earned the right to boast about their sustainable building practices as this thoughtfully created waterfront park takes shape out of what was not long ago an uninviting and polluted industrial waterfront.

72. QUEENS BOTANICAL GARDEN VISITOR & ADMINISTRATION BUILDING

The remarkable green roof on top of the Queens Botanical Garden's (QBG) Visitor & Administration Center and the building it covers earned numerous well-deserved accolades soon after it opened in 2007, including a LEED® Platinum rating (Leadership in Energy and Environmental Design), the highest rating given by the U.S. Green Building Council.

The QBG began as a five-acre exhibition at the 1939 World's Fair. Twenty-five years later, when Robert Moses, the famous "Master Builder" of New York City, was planning the 1964 World's Fair, he bartered the original 5-acre site for a nearby 39-acre site, which has since been the permanent home of the beloved QBG. In the 21st century, QBG has a mandate of environmental stewardship, and the gorgeous $27 million facility exemplifies this commitment.

Several features distinguish this 2,900 square foot green roof, some obvious and others hidden from view. The first unique feature is that this rooftop was imagined with access for all, with no stairs to climb, but rather a gently sloping, gravel ramp. Also, the roof garden is planted with native grasses and wildflowers, providing the right ecology for indigenous birds and butterflies. During a light rain, the green roof absorbs 100% of the precipitation but with heavier showers, the extra rainwater flows into the decorative ponds and fountains by the ground floor entrance, reducing polluted rainwater runoff by an astounding 95%. Finally, the green roof insulates the auditorium underneath it, keeping it warmer during winter and cooler during summer.

Queens Botanical Garden Visitor & Administration Building

Location: Flushing, Queens

Address: 43-50 Main St. Flushing, NY 11355

Phone: 718.886.3800

queensbotanical.org

Subway:

Subway Stop: Main St-Flushing

Calendar: Year-round Tue-Sun

Hours: Apr-Oct 8am-6pm, Nov-Mar 8am-4:30pm

$

Photo by Ari Burling

157

73. BRONX COUNTY COURTHOUSE

Hidden on top of the magnificent Classical Revival style Bronx County Courthouse, tucked behind a 10-foot parapet wall, is a little-known jewel: a 10,000 square foot green roof. The limestone and granite courthouse was completed in 1934, added to the National Register of Historical Places in 1983 and crowned with the first "extensive" (meaning that plants are grown in four inches of soil) green roof in the South Bronx in 2006. This was also the first green roof on any of the 53 New York City Department of Citywide Administration Services buildings.

This is a functioning courthouse for the New York State Supreme Court of Bronx County; visitors are required to submit to an extensive security check before being permitted to enter. A rule to be aware of: while you may enter with your cell phone, even if it has a camera feature, no cameras that function only as cameras are allowed.

Once inside, take the elevator to the ninth floor and follow the signs to the green roof. While the public is allowed to visit, be aware that you will be walking past courthouse employees' offices during business hours, so please show proper courtesy.

Open the unassuming ninth floor door to discover the courthouse's hidden living treasure. The roof was planted primarily with multiple varieties of flowering sedum plants in shallow lightweight soil. But the designer added deeper growing medium through the length of this rectangular green roof in the shape of a dramatic wave where tall meadow grasses reach several feet in height. You may also notice some electronic equipment in the midst of the green roof where scientific data is being collected to quantify benefits of the green roof, such as storm water absorption and cooler roof temperatures.

The parapet wall surrounding the green roof protects the plants from wind but, unfortunately, it also blocks views of the Grand Concourse, Yankee Stadium and Manhattan that would otherwise be visible.

Bronx County Courthouse

Location: South Bronx

Address: 851 Grand Concourse, Bronx, NY 10451

Subway:

Ⓑ Ⓓ ④

Subway Stop: 161st St-Yankee Stadium

Calendar: Year-round

Hours: Mon-Fri 9am-4pm

Free

Photo by Ari Burling

Fort Schuyler

Location: Bronx

Address: 6 Pennyfield Ave.
Throgs Neck, Bronx, NY
10465

Phone: 718.409.7200

sunymaritime.edu/
MaritimeMuseum/
FortSchuyler/

Subway:

Subway Stop: Westchester
Square Station, then BX40
Fort Schuyler bus

Best way to get there: Car

Calendar: Year-round

Hours: Mon-Sat 9am-4pm

Free

Photo by Ari Burling

74. FORT SCHUYLER (BRONX)

Only the most determined roof explorers are likely to
experience this history-laden living roof as it strategically
resides at the very top of the Bronx on a narrow land-spit,
now known as Throgs Neck. Yet those willing to make the
journey will be well-rewarded.

Fort Schuyler, adjacent to the Throgs Neck Bridge where
the Long Island Sound and the East River meet, was built
after the War of 1812 to protect New York from a foreign
water invasion. The fort played multiple roles in the Civil
War as a jail for prisoners of war, a hospital and a training
station before soldiers were deployed to the South.

The up-to-11-foot thick granite walls, exposed wooden beams and arched brickwork are lovingly cared for today as this is the campus of the renowned Maritime College, now run by State University of New York (SUNY). It is also the home of the fascinating Maritime Industry Museum, housing an extensive collection of boat models and treasures that ignite the imagination from the magical world of ships and shipping.

When exploring the campus grounds, look for the outdoor steps that lead to the fort's irregular pentagon-shaped rooftop. Built to house a huge armament, over time, this has included two enormous ten-inch and twelve-inch guns on disappearing carriages, strategically placed to protect the young Union from invaders. Today, the guns are gone, and a gorgeous grassy park with trees large enough to provide ample shade has taken root above the hefty stone walls and ceilings of this impressive 19th century historical structure.

75. FORT TOMPKINS QUADRANGLE & BATTERY WEED AT FORT WADSWORTH IN STATEN ISLAND

Fort Wadsworth, a strategic location on the southeastern shore of Staten Island, has guarded the entrance of New York Harbor since George Washington was president over 200 years ago. It has the distinction of being the fort with the longest continuous military use in the United States and is listed on the National Register of Historic Places. It is also the starting point for 50,000 runners for the annual New York City Marathon.

Within Fort Wadsworth are two green-roofed structures dating back to the mid-1800s. Directly on the harbor is Battery Weed, a catacomb-like, three-tiered granite structure capable of firing more than 116 cannons at once. This trapezoidal fortification lies on the water's edge where the Atlantic Ocean meets New York City Harbor.

On the bluff above, protecting Battery Weed, is the other green-roofed structure called Fort Tompkins. This was built as a barracks as well as a fortification. It has a fascinating design-

built rooftop water collection system for the soldiers living in the barracks. Today, this spectacular windy bluff above New York Harbor is home to plants and seeds that have managed to take root deposited by Mother Nature.

Fort Tompkins is not generally open to visitors, but if you catch one of the Park Rangers on a quiet day and express genuine interest in the Fort Tompkins rooftop, he or she may take you on a guided tour of the water cisterns inside the structure and perhaps even up to the roof to see where the water collection system begins.

To further explore the 226-acre fort, on certain full-moonlit nights and for a small fee, you can arrange to take the two-hour ranger-led "Lantern Tour." Plus, if you just can't face rushing back to the urban hustle and bustle, Fort Wadsworth now offers overnight camping.

Fort Tompkins Quadrangle and Battery Weed

Location: Within Fort Wadsworth, along the northeastern shores of Staten Island

Address: 210 New York Ave, Staten Island, NY 10305

Phone: 718.354.4500

nyharborparks.org

Best way to get there: Staten Island Ferry then bicycle, or Express Bus from Manhattan with a 10-minute walk

Calendar: Year-round

Hours: Wed-Sun 10am-4:30pm

Free

Photo by Ari Burling

THE TOWERS AT THE
WALDORF ASTORIA ROOF GARDEN

Growing food takes space, and urban farming has begun to take advantage of the available space a city has to offer: rooftops!

Growing edibles in everything from milk crates (Riverpark Farm) to manufactured lightweight soil (Brooklyn Grange at the Brooklyn Navy Yard) to high-tech hydroponic greenhouses (Whole Foods/Gotham Greens in Brooklyn), the farms in Section 5 are an exhilarating adventure in urban innovation.

SECTION 5:
ELEVATED FARMS

76. THE ROOFTOP KITCHEN GARDEN AT THE CROSBY STREET HOTEL

It's no surprise that this perfectly delightful boutique inn, the Crosby Street Hotel, extends its inimitable style to its charming rooftop mini-farm. Although the farm is not normally open to the public, the hotel will accommodate special requests for a private tour of this twelfth floor, chef-curated rooftop vegetable (and much more) patch.

Crosby restaurant offerings such as focaccia with rosemary and olive oil, eggs poached in heirloom tomatoes with herbed goat cheese toast, tempura battered zucchini blossoms, summer squash soup with herb pesto and tagliatelle with courgettes, wilted arugula and shaved pecorino taste even more delicious when made with the produce grown on the roof each summer.

In this manageably sized garden, 15 blueberry bushes yield about 15 gallons of blueberries during the month of July alone. Delectable heirloom tomatoes with fabulous names like "Limony," "Big Rainbow," "Green Zebra" and "Aunt Ruby's Green" as well as basil, rosemary and other herbs are grown alongside arugula and edible flowers. What looks like a Tudor-style dollhouse is actually a chicken coop for four beautiful Araucana chickens that lay blue-shelled eggs daily.

This small, attractive garden is an inspiration to wannabe urban roof farmers, and a hidden treasure for those who love visiting innovative rooftops.

Plus be sure to enjoy the Crosby's other rooftop garden on the second floor. Entering this garden is only for guests staying in the "Meadow Suite," but all hotel visitors and guests can see into the "American Woodland Meadow." Accurately named, it is planted with over 50 varieties of native plants, creating a true miniature native woodland.

The Rooftop Kitchen Garden

Location: SoHo

Address: 79 Crosby St. NY, NY 10012, between Spring and Prince St.

Phone: 212.226.6400

firmdalehotels.com/new-york/crosby-street-hotel

Subway:

6

Subway Stop: Spring St.

Calendar: Late spring, summer and early fall

Hours: By appointment

Reservations: Yes

Free

Photo courtesy of The Crosby Street Hotel

77. ROSEMARY'S

This wildly popular enoteca (wine bar with small plates) and trattoria (a rustic, family owned Italian restaurant) has an inviting, bucolic appeal with tiles, exposed bricks, natural wood and lots of light, plus al fresco sidewalk seating in warm weather. But best of all, up one flight of easy-to-climb stairs, is Rosemary's rooftop farm where micro greens, tomatoes, berries, peppers and herbs, including, of course, fragrant rosemary, are grown from late spring throughout summer and into early fall.

Rosemary's owner, who runs another popular restaurant close by, has a real stake in the West Village neighborhood. He has partnered with three community organizations, two of which are rooftop-centric. The first partner, an elementary school around the corner called PS41, has a student-accessible, $1.7 million sedum rooftop. Another partner, The Brooklyn Grange, New York's original commercial rooftop farmers, helped Rosemary's create this "mini-Grange" rooftop farm using the same materials and methods.

All this community-mindedness results in the freshest and most delicious ingredients in your traditionally prepared Italian food, as if you had been transported to a small Tuscan bistro with its own kitchen garden. But since you are actually in New York City where there is no room for a traditional in-ground garden, this patch just happens to be planted on the rooftop.

Rosemary's

Location: Greenwich Village

Address: 18 Greenwich Ave. NY, NY 10011, at W. 10th St.

Phone: 212.647.1818

rosemarysnyc.com

Subway:

Subway Stop: West 4th Street

Calendar: Spring, summer and early fall growing seasons

Hours: Mon-Fri 8am-4:30pm and 5pm-midnight, Sat and Sun 10am-4pm. and 5pm-midnight

Reservations: Only for large groups

$$$

Photos by Heather Shimmin

Riverpark Farm at Alexandria Center™

Location: Kips Bay

Address: 450 E. 29th St. NY, NY 10016, east of First Ave.

Phone: 212.729.9790

riverparkfarm.com

Subway:

Subway Stop: 6 to 28th St, then a long walk or L to 1st Ave. then a long walk

Best way to get there: M9 bus or bicycle

Calendar: May-October

Hours: Free farm tours each Tue at 12:30pm

Free

Photos by Heather Shimmin

78. RIVERPARK FARM AT ALEXANDRIA CENTER™

Today's sophisticated diners have experienced farm-to-table dinin but at Riverpark, the superb restaurant adjacent to Riverpark Far Alexandria Center™, diners enjoy a unique urban variation: crate plate dining.

Situated on the roof of an unseen parking garage, a sea of doubl stacked milk crates, the top one carefully lined with a special fab and filled with rich, compost-laden soil, make-up the 3,200 cubic of growing space at Riverpark Farm. A mind-boggling 165 varietie of edibles were grown in portable one-foot-by-one-foot plastic cra during the summer of 2012, and more than 5,000 pounds of care planned produce was harvested from this movable farm during its season, all of it used exclusively by Riverpark's talented chefs.

During the winter season, Chef Sisha Ortúzar and his team comp their farmers market wish list. Based on that, Zach Pickens, an extraordinarily innovative urban farmer, creates the growing plan implements it, step by step, so that early in the season, the chef-requested berries, herbs, greens, vegetables, roots, edible flowe and a huge variety of heirloom tomatoes are available. After bein picked each morning, the harvest is delivered across the plaza to kitchen to fulfill the delicious promises of that day's menu.

Free farm tours are available each Tuesday at 12:30 p.m., no reservations necessary. Family-style farm dinners are served outdoors on the rooftop terrace for groups of 6-12; this one-of-a- Manhattan culinary experience requires a reservation and a heft credit limit.

79. THE TOWERS OF THE WALDORF ASTORIA ROOFTOP GARDEN

The storied art-deco masterpiece that takes up an entire city block between Park and Lexington Avenues, between E. 49th and E. 50th Streets has a new surprise on its rooftop, or at least on the sprawling 20th floor setback.

With the help of the Horticultural Society of New York and the New York Restoration Project, almost one-third of this 25,000 square foot rooftop has already been transformed into a garden and the highest apiary (a collection of beehives) in Manhattan. Six hives housing about 60,000 worker bees toil away at their prestigious midtown residence. In order to make sure the bees have plenty to nibble on, the Waldorf has installed eight raised planter beds growing berries, flowers, squash, lavender, and herbs galore, as well as several containers growing figs and eight varieties of apples.

The chefs in the restaurants, the mixologists at the bars and the clinicians in the top-notch hotel spa use everything rooftop: royal jelly and lavender in the spa, herbs at the bars and squash blossoms and berries in the restaurants. Spa, restaurants and bars all use the coveted "Top of the Waldorf" honey.

If having guests on the rooftop of the Waldorf seems like a new idea, it isn't. The original Waldorf-Astoria on Fifth Avenue and 34th Street, where the Empire State Building now stands, boasted an elegant rooftop garden. So in 1931, when the hotel was rebuilt on this site, the 20th floor setback was indeed designed for guests' enjoyment. Over time, as the hotel deteriorated along with New York City as a whole, the rooftop was relegated to a much less glamorous function: housing heating and air conditioning units. Restoration of the grand property began in the 1980s and finally, in 2012, renovation reached the rooftop, restoring and possibly improving upon the original intended use of this glorious open-air space with Waldorf Astoria-worthy views.

The Towers of the Waldorf Astoria Rooftop Garden

Location: Midtown

Address: 301 Park Ave. NY, NY 10022, at E. 49th St.

Phone: 212.355.3000

towersofthewaldorfastoria.com

Subway

6

Subway Stop: 51st St.

Calendar: Summer growing season

Hours: Thu and Sat tours with lunch

Reservations: Yes

$$$

Photos by Heather Shimmin

Riverbank State Park Community Garden

Location: Harlem

Address: 679 Riverside Dr. NY, NY 10031; entrances at W. 138th St. and W. 145th St.

Phone: 212.694.3600

nysparks.com/parks/93/details.aspx

Subway:

Subway Stop: 137th St. or 145th St.

Calendar: Apr-Dec

Hours: 7am-8pm

Free

Photos by Heather Shimmin

80. RIVERBANK STATE PARK COMMUNITY GARDEN

Early each spring, with the tumble of the bingo wheel, the lottery for coveted plots in the Riverbank State Park's community garden takes place. Only 59 lucky players win the privilege of growing fruits, flowers, vegetables and herbs in this unique elevated garden situated 69 feet above the Hudson River.

Anyone can enter the free lottery, but residents in the two Hamilton Heights zip codes surrounding the park get to enter twice, doubling their chances. Winners sign an actual gardening contract, promising they will tend their plot regularly, compost their waste, clean up after themselves and be good garden plot neighbors. If the rules are broken, the next lucky person on the wait list steps in and takes over midseason for the duration of the contract.

From that point forward, the winning gardeners can be as creative or practical as they like. As long as what is planted stays within the bounds of the assigned garden plot, they can grow edibles or ornamentals, or any combination they fancy in this one-of-a-kind urban rooftop community garden.

81. 5 BORO GREEN ROOF GARDEN

The largest multi-system green roof on the planet exists in what is probably the quietest part of Manhattan, Randall's Island. Atop the New York City Parks Five Borough Administrative Building, 30 different green roof systems covering 30,000 square feet grow side by side.

Different types and depths of growing medium are planted with native plants, a variety of sedum, fruits, vegetables, herbs and berries. There is a hydroponic system and even a solar green roof. Thousands of Italian honey bees living in the apiary buzz around, happily pollinating the plants. Up to 6,000 gallons of rainwater overflow is captured in barrels to reduce storm water runoff, and is later used to irrigate the roof garden. With so much experimentation going on, progress in this massive green roof laboratory is carefully documented to determine what works best in green roof systems.

This living roof encourages biodiversity in animals and insects, plus it creates a beautiful park-like setting for bipeds (that's us) to spend time enjoying the views of the East River, the Triborough (Robert F. Kennedy) Bridge, and the unique vistas available only from this island-bound green roof laboratory.

The roof resides atop an unassuming limestone structure that now serves as the New York City Parks Department Five Borough Administration Building. Originally called, simply, "The Administration Building," it was built to specification by the most powerful man in 20th-century New York City, Robert Moses, the "Master Builder." In 1937, Moses moved into the office he placed very near the toll booth for one of his most ambitious and profitable projects, The Triborough Bridge. As the Triborough Bridge and Tunnel Authority chairman, Moses could just about hear drivers' coins drop into the toll booth collectors tank, adding up to millions of dollars and more power for Moses and his Authority.

In 1989, long after Moses' decades-long reign was curtailed by Governor Nelson A. Rockefeller, the building was renamed and repurposed as a headquarters for the NYC Parks Department. In 2007, in response to Mayor Bloomberg's comprehensive sustainability plan, the Parks Department installed the first 7,000 square feet of this green roof. Each year, under the loving care of Artie Rollins (Assistant Commission of Citywide Services for the Parks Department) and his attentive staff, another carefully chosen green roof system or two is added to expand the unique information being collected.

Available only by prearranged tour, and with limited bus service to Randall's Island, this destination is for roof explorers who are excellent planners and in no rush.

5 Boro Green Roof Garden

Location: Randall's Island

Address: New York City Parks Department Five Borough (5-Boro) Administration Building, Randall's Island, NY 10035

Phone: 212.360.8905

Arthur.Rollins@parks.nyc.gov

Subway:

4 5 6

Subway Stop: 125th St. then walk across footbridge or take M35 bus

Calendar: Year-round

Hours: Mon-Fri 9am-5pm

Reservations: By appointment only

Free

Photo by Ari Burling

Location: 44 Eagle St.
Brooklyn, NY 11222

rooftopfarms.org

Subway:

Subway Stop: Greenpoint
Ave.

Calendar: Growing season

Hours: Sun 1pm-4pm

Free

Photo by Ari Burling

82. EAGLE STREET ROOFTOP FARM

While rooftop farms seem to be popping up all over, New York City's first commercial, open-air, soil-based rooftop farm was begun in 2009 on the roof of Broadway Stages, an unassuming warehouse-style building near the shore of the East River in Greenpoint, Brooklyn.

Ben Flanner (of Brooklyn Grange fame) and Annie Novak transformed this 60 x 100 rooftop into a commercial farm that provides bicycle-delivered produce to local restaurants as well as rooftop-fresh produce to the community through its weekly farm stand and CSA (Community Supported Agriculture). Eagle Street Rooftop Farm also functions as an education hub, where children learn about nutrition, plus the farm is a pivotal community partner with an active roster of urban farmer trainees, interns and apprentices.

Each Sunday during the growing season, from 1-4 p.m., visitors are welcomed to this organic farm with its tidy rows of greens, peppers, tomatoes, eggplants, kale, lettuce and carrots interspersed with cheerful, natural insect-battling marigolds. Trainees, some of them mirroring Annie's style, wear flowing long skirts and lovingly tend the garden while a few tourists and the occasional photographer wander through, carefully stepping between the mounded rows of lightweight growing medium.

At center stage of this picturesque farm in the sky is a chicken coop on wheels housing three gorgeous birds who garner much attention from camera-toting urban eco-tourists. To up the adorable factor even more, the farm's rabbits are let out occasionally to hop around and make their valuable fertilizer contribution to the farm as well. Joining in on the biodiversity bandwagon is a beehive on the roof elevation just below the farm, and according to Annie, these pollinators are an integral part of the farm, dramatically increasing the yield of produce.

During the growing season, the weekly Eagle Street farm stand offers their rooftop honey, hot sauce made from their roof-grown peppers, plus veggies and herbs, all grown, harvested and prepared without ever having traveled via fossil-fuel burning transportation. It is no wonder Eagle Street Rooftop Farm is widely recognized as a prime example of urban rooftop farming.

Location: Wallabout, Brooklyn

Address: Brooklyn Navy Yard, Building 3, 11th Floor, Brooklyn NY 11205

brooklyngrangefarm.com

facebook.com/
brooklyngrange

instragram.com/
brooklyngrange

Subway:

Subway Stop: A/C to High St-Brooklyn Bridge or F to York St.

Calendar: May-Nov

Hours: Please check website

Free

Photo by Ari Burling

83. BROOKLYN GRANGE FARM AT THE BROOKLYN NAVY YARD

At the 300-acre Brooklyn Navy Yard, with its 150-year history of shipbuilding, there is one sky-bound acre in particular that stands out – the Brooklyn Grange Rooftop Farm. On the massive rooftop of Building 3, 11 stories above Wallabout Bay, is the world's largest commercial rooftop farm.

The Brooklyn Navy Yard farm is not only an environmentally sustainable business, but also an economically sustainable one. In fact, Brooklyn Grange exemplifies the "Triple Bottom Line": it is financially profitable, socially responsible and environmentally sustainable. The hard work performed by the innovators at Brooklyn

Grange feeds the bodies and nourishes the souls of their neighbors who share a love for healthy living and New York City.

But there is even more benefit to the City from this 65,000 square foot farm. It manages over one million gallons of storm water annually. That means more than one million gallons of waste water each year will not go into the overburdened and aging sewer system because of this single rooftop farm. It is no wonder the Department of Environmental Protection (DEP) awarded Brooklyn Grange a sizeable grant to help transform this roof into the agricultural oasis it is.

Unlike many commercial farms, the beautiful Brooklyn Grange welcomes visitors and trainees. Each week during the growing season, there are open times for self-guided tours. Weekly sunset yoga classes are taught amongst the sweet-smelling herbs. Celebratory farm dinners take place for events and organizations. School groups visit the Grange to learn first-hand about compost, worms and bees.

Although this rooftop is a little off the beaten track, it is one that must be seen – and tasted – to be believed.

84. GOTHAM GREENS ROOFTOP FARM AT WHOLE FOODS MARKET®

If innovation and adaptation are keys to a city's vitality, then no place is more vital than 21st century Brooklyn rooftops. With the latest greenhouse technology, it is now possible to serve arugula tonight that was harvested this morning on the rooftop where you did your marketing today.

Whole Foods Market®, a nationwide chain of natural food stores, has partnered with Gotham Greens, a group of Brooklyn-based urban agriculture experts that farm exclusively in ultra-high-tech rooftop greenhouses. The result is a 20,000 square foot, hydroponic, pesticide-free, temperature-controlled, sustainably farmed rooftop greenhouse, a first in a national grocery chain.

Remarkably, the greenhouse isn't the only fabulous rooftop amenity Whole Foods Market® is offering its food-centric Brooklyn customers. On the second floor is a casual eatery appropriately named "The Roof." Overlooking the Gowanus Canal, this indoor-outdoor cafe offers an array of craft beers on tap and a menu of locally sourced dishes, including vegan and vegetarian options.

Emerging neighborhoods often have stark contrasts between their industrial past and their high-tech future, and Gowanus is no exception. Super-choosey Brooklynite foodies are enjoying the ultimate in sustainably farmed produce grown right next to the most toxic waterway in the country. The good news is new technology will soon be helping sort out the centuries-old Gowanus Canal mess with a half-billion dollar dredging project scheduled to begin in 2016.

Gotham Greens Rooftop Farm at Whole Foods Market®

Location: Gowanus, Brooklyn

Address: 214 3rd St. Brooklyn, NY 11215

Phone: 718.907.3622

Hours: 8am-11pm daily

wholefoodsmarket.com/stores/brooklyn

Subway:

D N R

Subway Stop: Union St.

Calendar: Year-round

Hours: 11am-11pm daily

Free

Photos by Heather Shimmin

Farm-in-the-Sky

Location: Bushwick, Brooklyn

Address: 214 Starr St. Brooklyn, NY 11237

ecostationny.com

Subway:

Subway Stop: Jefferson St.

Calendar: Late spring through early fall

Hours: Varies

Reservations: Yes

Free

Photo by Sharokh Mirzai

85. FARM-IN-THE-SKY (FITS)

Created from a glorious hodgepodge of recycled buckets, burlap bags, storage bins and cola bottles, Farm-in-the-Sky is on a mission to bring urban farming to the masses. Using just about anything that's free and food-safe, the farmers-in-the-sky plant herbs, micro greens, peppers, tomatoes, kale, and more for a total of 30 kinds of produce for their local restaurant partners and farmer's market in "upcycled" containers, things that otherwise would have been considered trash.

Farm-in-the-Sky's purpose is to simplify the process of rooftop farming, and then teach community members how cheap, easy and delicious it is to grow the freshest, healthiest food possible on their own rooftop or terrace, or even in window boxes.

Programs and tour times vary so contact FITS before heading out to Bushwick, and plan to stay and enjoy a bite at the street-level café that uses the delicious roof-grown produce.

86. BROOKLYN GRANGE FLAGSHIP FARM IN LONG ISLAND CITY, QUEENS

A lot of calculations need to be made when creating a commercially-viable rooftop farm. How much manufactured lightweight soil is needed to create 150 rows that are 10-inches deep? How many seedlings need to be started? Which varieties should be planted? How long does it take for each plant to be ready for picking? The questions barely begin there, which is why, at one of the world's largest rooftop farms, the spreadsheet is equally important as the shovel and the hoe.

Around 2008, a young man with a twinkle in his eye, a degree in industrial engineering and a particular talent for advising businesses on efficiency via the magic of spreadsheet analysis became enamored of farming, yet he wanted to stay in Brooklyn. Because the only undeveloped New York City urban spaces large enough to grow food are on tops of buildings, he began his search for an appropriate rooftop. Unfathomable dedication, team work, countless spreadsheets and lots of luck later, in 2010, the (then) world's largest rooftop farm, at about one acre, was unveiled. Ben Flanner and his partners succeeded in bringing commercial farming back to New York City.

While growing hyper-local food for profit is the underlying goal of Brooklyn Grange Farm, the urban environment and community also profit enormously. In fact, Brooklyn Grange has been featured in newspapers, magazines, films, conferences and books worldwide, serving as a model for lifestyle-dedicated urbanites who now know that they can insist on access to the freshest possible, organically grown food.

Visitors and farmers market shoppers are welcome at Brooklyn Grange. Check their website for details.

**Brooklyn Grange
Flagship Farm**

Location: Long Island City,
Queens

Address: 37-18 Northern
Blvd. Long Island City, NY
11101

brooklyngrangfarm.com

facebook.com/
brooklyngrange

instragram.com/
brooklyngrange

Subway:

Ⓜ Ⓡ

Subway Stop: 36th St.

Calendar: approximately
May-Oct

Hours: Check website for
farm stand and visitor days

Free

Photo by Ari Burling

187

ANNUAL KITE FLIGHT

The jazz scene might lurk in underground clubs, but rooftop entertainment abounds in New York City.

Summertime film festivals (Rooftop Films and the Czech Center), flying trapeze lessons with a view (Trapeze School New York) and star gazing through an enormous telescope from the roof of the building where dozens of Nobel Prize winning physicists did their research (Columbia University's Pupin Hall) are just a few of the rooftop activities available that are as varied as the inhabitants of the city they serve.

SECTION 6:
ROOFTOP CLASSES, ENTERTAINMENT AND SPORTS

Russian and Turkish Baths

Location: East Village

Address: 268 E. 10th St. NY, NY 10009, between First Ave. and Ave. A

Phone: 212.674.9250

russianandturkishbaths. com

Subway:

Subway Stop: First Ave.

Best way to get there: M8 Bus

Calendar: Year-round

Hours: Co-ed: Mon, Tue, Fri noon-10pm, Sat 9am-10pm, Sun 2pm-10pm. Women only: Wed 10am-2pm. Men only: Thur noon-5pm, Sun 8am-2pm

$$

Photo by Heather Shimmin

87. RUSSIAN AND TURKISH BATHS

Step into this unassuming row house on East 10th Street and you walk into a slice of New York City history. A piece of the old country was transported to the New World at a time when poor Eastern European Jewish immigrants filled the shoddy East Village tenements to overflowing. This is the unique context of the Russian and Turkish Baths. Since the late 19th century, this downtown institution has been a living relic of the pervasive Yiddish culture when men went to the baths to "schvitz" and "kibbitz" (sweat and chat).

This explains why the small, second floor sundeck is as unadorned as the rest of the storied Russian and Turkish Baths. Regardless of the celebrity-studded guest list that recently has included Colin Farrell, P Diddy and Tyne Daly, there is no pretention on the roof deck, or anywhere in the 120-plus-year-old bathhouse.

Since 1892, men (and more recently women) have been coming to this East Village location to sweat their way to health in one of the few purpose-built 200-degree Russian rooms in the country. Twenty thousand pounds of rocks are cooked overnight in order to radiate a hot, steamy, intense heat all day long. The milder Turkish, aromatherapy steam and redwood sauna rooms are also available, as is the bracing 46-degree plunge pool to instantly revive you between treatment rooms.

Since bath house admission is sold as a day pass, you can refresh yourself for another cycle of hot rooms with a nap or a smoke on the roof deck. But before heading back down to the basement for another fabulous round of heat, notice the idiosyncratic backyard view. A private glimpse into the surrounding, fully occupied, century-old apartment buildings allows for an unusual window into the past in this historic immigrant neighborhood.

88. TRAPEZE SCHOOL NEW YORK

One of the most thrilling rooftop activities in New York City is taking a class in the "aerial arts" at Trapeze School New York. "Turn your brain off and leave it all behind"—that's the attraction to flying on the Pier 40 rooftop rig, according to Toni Machi, one of the delightful TSNY instructors. The building on which classes take place is several stories tall, so another attraction is the elevated view of the adjacent river with watercraft wending their way up and down the mighty Hudson.

Classes in the flying trapeze are available to just about anyone who is able to overcome the fear of climbing up the rope ladder to a small platform, holding onto the bar and jumping off 25 feet above this riverside rooftop. According to TSNY, anyone, athletic or not, age 6 or older, and who weighs less than 205 pounds, can safely learn and practice the basics of flying trapeze in their two-hour group classes. For the rooftop adventure of a lifetime, you must try this.

Trapeze School New York

Location: Hudson River Park, Pier 40 roof

Address: 353 West St. NY, NY 10014

Phone: 212.242.8769

trapezeschool.com

Subway:

Subway Stop: Houston St.

Calendar: May-Oct

Hours: Class times vary

Reservations: Yes

$$

Photo by Ari Burling

89. THE RED SHIRT ROOFTOP READING SERIES

A few minutes walk east of the storied Chelsea Hotel, where emerging artists once lived, thrived and sometimes died, a 21st-century organization to celebrate diverse emerging artists was begun. Red Shirt Entertainment, under the inclusive, warm embrace of Producing Artistic Director, Rajendra Ramoon Maharaj, has created an annual three-day theater event on their cozy Flatiron District rooftop.

Before the plays are presented, prepare to be mesmerized by this urban setting, with the Flatiron Building close enough for you to enjoy its exquisite detail, and scores of iconic New York City cedar water tanks in plain sight. With this romantic view of Manhattan as the backdrop, the Red Shirt Entertainment Rooftop Reading Series showcases ten 10-minute plays by a diverse group of emerging artists over one gorgeous summer New York City weekend. (As roof explorers, we have to be perpetually optimistic about the weather forecast.)

For those who love edgy, experimental theater and want to be part of what very well could be "the next big thing," Red Shirt's Rooftop Reading Series is a way to be up close and personal with the writers, directors and actors at this annual intimate rooftop event. Seating is limited so book early, and show up early too, to enjoy the positive urban vibe surrounding this Flatiron District rooftop.

The Red Shirt Rooftop Reading Series

Location: Flatiron District

Address: 18 W. 23rd St. NY, NY 10010

Phone: 212.389.9782

redshirtentertainment.com

Subway:

N **R**

Subway Stop: 23rd St.

Calendar: One weekend in September

Hours: Fri and Sat night, Sun afternoon

Reservations: Yes

$

Photos by Heather Shimmin

90. MIDTOWN TENNIS CLUB

From mid-May through late September, boost your vitamin D level while indulging in some outdoor rooftop tennis at the Midtown Tennis Club. The "speakeasy" of tennis facilities, Midtown Tennis Club's entrance, next to a McDonald's and a Gristedes grocery store, is so unassuming you might just miss it. Not only is it well-hidden, the name is also misleading. The Midtown Tennis Club is located in Chelsea rather than Midtown, and this "club" does not require a membership to play. At least the word "tennis" in the tagline is accurate.

The nearly half-century-old tennis club was the first to offer indoor and rooftop tennis to Manhattanites. Each spring, they take down the giant grey bubble covering the four rooftop

Midtown Tennis Club

Location: Chelsea

Address: 341 Eighth Ave. NY, NY 10001, at W. 27th St.

Phone: 212.989.8572

midtowntennis.com

Subway:

Subway Stop: 23rd St.

Calendar: May-Sept

Hours: Mon-Fri 7am-11pm, Sat and Sun 8am-10pm

Reservations: Yes

$$-$$$

Photo by Rhea Alexander

courts. The bumpy clay surface with the infamously short 12-foot backcourt might present a few challenges, but the location can't be beat, the rates are attractive, and the clientele is often studded with bigwigs from the fashion industry working on their backhand and killer serve before heading to the office.

Empire State Building

Location: Midtown

Address: 350 Fifth Ave. NY, NY 10018, at 34th St.

Phone: 212.736.3100

esb.nyc.com

Subway:

Subway Stop: 34th St-Herald Square

Calendar: Year-round

Hours: 8am-2am daily

Reservations: Recommended

$$

Photo by Ari Burling

91. EMPIRE STATE BUILDING 86TH FLOOR OBSERVATION DECK

There is more than one way to get to the top of the Empire State Building.

Perhaps the most famous visitor to the Observation Deck, the 1933 fictional giant ape named King Kong, was never really there. In this early Hollywood action film, Kong climbed the exterior of the world's then-tallest skyscraper. The Empire State Building, synonymous with New York City and having held the title as the tallest building in the world for 40 years, has been in scores of Hollywood movies since King Kong, making it the most recognizable skyscraper in the world.

Alternatively, in the real-yet-hard-to-believe world, one law-breaking daredevil chose to replicate Kong's adventure. In 1994, the "French Spiderman," Alain Robert, climbed the outside of the building to the 86th floor without any climbing or safety equipment.

For those who prefer a more secure journey to the Observation Deck, join the more than 110 million visitors who have taken the high-speed elevators to the 86th floor. This still-thrilling method is safe, fast and easy, especially when visitors buy tickets to this popular attraction in advance.

Finally, there is another, legal, way to climb the world's most recognized skyscraper – take the stairs! Since 1978, one day each February, hundreds of athletes race up the 1,576 steps, with a record time under 10 minutes. This annual charity event is organized by New York Road Runners.

Whether you ride the elevators today, or plan to run up her steps next February, make sure to experience the (for now) tallest New York City roof terrace, the Empire State Building's 86th Floor Observation Deck.

Location: Midtown

Address: 30 Rockefeller Plaza, NY, NY 10112, 50th St. between Fifth and Sixth Ave.

Phone: 212.698.2000

topoftherocknyc.com

Subway:

Subway Stop: 47-50 St-Rockefeller Center

Calendar: Year-round

Hours: 8am-midnight daily

Reservations: Recommended

$$

Photos by Arlene Bender

92. TOP OF THE ROCK®

Rockefeller Center is the 22-acre complex that includes 14 elegant Art Deco buildings erected during the Great Depression, between 1930-1938. The rooftop of the 70-story centerpiece is open to the public. Originally known as the RCA Building, and now known as the GE Building or "30 Rock," it is the jewel in the Rockefeller Center crown. The observation deck on the 70th floor mesmerizes visitors with a 360-degree vista of New York City from one indoor and two outdoor observation decks.

It also offers the only public view of the five Italianate roof gardens at Rockefeller Center atop the British Empire Building and La Maison Francaise. These opulent oases are some of the oldest Manhattan roof gardens still in existence. They were open to the public briefly, from 1935-1938, but since then have been seen only by the fortunate tenants of the buildings above them, or to the privileged few who pay hefty fees to rent these hidden Midtown gardens for their private soirees.

John D. Rockefeller started life with nothing and, through brains, hard work and grit, became America's first billionaire. He and his son, John D. Rockefeller, Jr., loved New York City and bestowed much of their public generosity locally. The opportunity to see the Rockefeller family's treasured New York City from 70 stories high is an ongoing gift the progeny of this shrewd businessman and renowned philanthropist gave to all of us who love the Big Apple.

93. ANNUAL KITE FLIGHT AT THE PORT AUTHORITY BUS TERMINAL

Kids of all ages will love this annual rooftop event. On a perfect fall day, everyone is invited to launch a colorful kite among dozens of others on the expansive seventh floor roof deck of the Port Authority parking garage. When the wind picks up, suddenly the sky is filled. The glass-clad Theater District skyscrapers surrounding this transformed parking lot reflect scores of flying, multicolored, diamond-shaped dots. Be sure to join the fun for the most urban kite flying opportunity of the year.

At this entirely free family event, sponsored by The Fashion Center Business Improvement District, kites are free, as is food, live music, jugglers, mimes, unicyclists, and a puppet show. Plus, an incredibly creative team of face painters is on hand to make sure everyone has a memorable day.

The Fashion Center Business Improvement District's Annual Kite Flight takes place the third or fourth Sunday each September on the seventh floor roof deck of the Port Authority Bus Terminal's Parking Lot. Enter the building at Eighth Avenue and W. 40th Street, turn left and take the elevator to the seventh floor. From 1 to 4 p.m. Free!

Annual Kite Flight

Location: Port Authority Bus Terminal rooftop

Address: Eighth Ave. at W. 40th St.

Phone: 212.764.9600

garmentdistrictnyc.com

Subway:

Ⓐ Ⓒ Ⓔ

Subway Stop: 42nd Street-Port Authority

Calendar: Third or fourth Sunday in September

Hours: 1pm-4pm

Free

Photos by Heather Shimmin

YoYoga!

Location: Midtown East

Address: 344 E. 59th St. 3rd Floor, NY, NY 10022, at Second Ave.

Phone: 646.490.7790

yoyoganyc.com

Subway:

N Q R 4 5 6

Subway Stop: N/Q/R to Lexington Ave/59th St. or 4/5/6 to 59th St.

Calendar: When temperature is 68 degrees or above

Hours: Check website

Reservations: Yes

$$

Photos by Heather Shimmin

94. YOYOGA!

When the mercury hits 68 degrees, it's rooftop yoga season at YoYoga! In good weather, classes move from the charming indoor third floor studio to the 1,300 square foot outdoor roof deck. The artificial turf-covered ground might be a little uneven, but the classes are a solid Hatha/Vinyasa blend taught by a rotating roster of kind, patient and experienced yogis.

The YoYoga! studio, located under the Queensboro Bridge, is run by a brother-sister team: Rebecca teaches classes while Kennedy works the desk. Both are warm and welcoming, and make the sincere effort to learn students' names. One gets the feeling that everyone at YoYoga! is part of the family.

If it is too lovely to stay inside and your body is telling you that it is time to enjoy all the mind-body benefits of an hour-long yoga session, head to the friendly little studio with the roof deck classes under the Queensboro Bridge.

95. BOHEMIAN NATIONAL HALL ROOFTOP TERRACE

In 2008, the century-plus old Bohemian National Hall reopened after a complete renovation from the ground floor up to and including the rooftop terrace. While they preserved the original Renaissance Revival façade and the elegant 19th century ballroom, the rest of the five-story building is very 21st century, with all the mod-cons, including an elevator that whisks visitors right up to the roof terrace.

In 2008, the Czech Center New York moved into the Hall to join the original tenant of the building, the Bohemian Benevolent and Literary Society, as well as the Consulate General of the Czech Republic. This co-tenancy makes this surviving ethnic social hall truly the starting point for all things Czech and Slovak in New York City.

Each Tuesday night throughout July and August, the Czech Center sponsors a film festival, now called "Czech That Film." The festival consists of about ten films, all in Czech with English subtitles. While most are current features, some old classics are thrown in. Screenings begin when the sun goes down, but the doors open at 7 p.m. so there is time to socialize and buy a drink from the rooftop kiosk before settling into one of the outdoor bistro-like chairs. Attendance used to be free of charge, but the rooftop film festival became so popular that a ticketing policy was started to ensure everyone gets a seat.

For those on a budget seeking a unique cultural event in a gorgeous historical building on a delightful modern rooftop, there is no better way to spend your summer Tuesday evenings.

Bohemian National Hall Rooftop Terrace

Location: Upper East Side

Address: 321 E. 73rd St. NY, NY 10021 between First and Second Ave.

Phone: 646.422.3399

czechcenter.org

Subway:

Subway Stop: 68th St-Hunter College

Calendar: July-Sept

Hours: Doors open at 7pm

Reservations: Yes

$

Photo by Heather Shimmin

Location: Yorkville

Address: 555 E. 90th St. NY, NY 10128, between York and East End Ave.

Phone: 212.369.8890

asphaltgreen.org

Subway:
4 5 6

Subway Stop: 86th St.

Best way to get there: M86 bus

Calendar: Late spring to early fall

Hours: Mon-Fri 5:30am-10pm, Sat-Sun 8am-8pm

$$

Photo by Heather Shimmin

96. ASPHALT GREEN ROOFTOP TERRACE

Where they once mixed asphalt, they now make athletes.

A century ago, the now-tony Yorkville section of the Upper East Side was an industrial zone and this site, adjacent to the East River, was selected to mix asphalt. Materials could be delivered by ship rather than truck, plus the river was dredged for sand and gravel, more of the required road-building ingredients. The Municipal Asphalt Plant, as it came to be known, continued to operate until 1968.

In its place today stands a five-and-a-half acre massive indoor and outdoor athletic complex that boasts the only 50-meter Olympic swimming pool in Manhattan. In fact, Lia Neal, the second African-American female to make the Olympic swim team, trained here from age 8. On top of the building where Lia swam is a large roof terrace with views that span the East River and into Queens.

Lounging on the spacious rooftop terrace, either in sun or shade, is a fabulous reward after, before, or in lieu of a terrific workout at this sprawling athletic facility. Bring a lock and towel and, if you plan to swim in one of the pools, be sure to pack a bathing cap.

97. THE RUTHERFORD OBSERVATORY (PUPIN HALL ROOFTOP AT COLUMBIA UNIVERSITY)

The most thrilling sight from most 15-story Manhattan rooftops is the view of the city below. But what the Rutherford Observatory, atop Pupin Hall at Columbia University, offers is the view above. It can outshine even New York City with some heavy-hitting celestial competition.

The view below includes the cathedral spires of the Union Theological Seminary and the George Washington Bridge, and is indeed spectacular. Yet the crowd is drawn here every other Friday for the opportunity to look up toward the planets, stars and constellations.

The Columbia Astronomy Public Outreach program holds a lecture/stargazing event twice a month during the academic year. The 30-minute lecture is followed by rooftop telescope observations, usually through one of three telescopes manned by the endearingly enthusiastic Columbia astronomy student volunteers. Inside the oxidized green rooftop dome, built well before the surrounding "light pollution" began interfering, is a 14-inch Meade Schmidt-Cassegrain telescope. The volunteers focus the telescope and remain on hand to answer questions.

While rooftop visitors explore the enormous wonders of the galaxy on top of Pupin Hall, its underground laboratories are where 29 Nobel Prize winners in physics studied the tiniest building blocks of our universe. In 1939, the first atom-splitting in the United States took place in the cyclotron in Pupin's basement. Furthermore, much of the early work on The Manhattan Project occurred at Pupin Physics Laboratories, and even our most famous wild-haired physicist, Einstein, did research here.

Take advantage of this opportunity to observe the heavens atop the building where the stars of the physics world have truly shined.

The Rutherford Observatory

Location: Morningside Heights on the Columbia University campus

Address: Pupin Hall, Columbia University Main Campus, NY, NY 10027.

Enter at 116th St. and Broadway, walk inside the campus to 120th St. and Broadway

Phone: 212.854.4608

outreach.astro.columbia.edu

Subway:

Subway Stop: 116th St.

Calendar: Alternate Fridays when classes are in session and the sky is clear (Sept-May)

Hours: Lectures at 7pm or 8pm, stargazing begins at dusk

Free

Photo by Heather Shimmin

CityView Racquet Club

Location: Long Island City, Queens

Address: 43-34 32nd Place, Long Island City, Queens, NY 11101

Phone: 718.389.6252

cityracquet.com

Subway:

Subway Stop: 33rd St/ Rawson

Calendar: Year-round

Hours: 6am-late

$$$

Photo courtesy of CityView Racquet Club

98. CITYVIEW RACQUET CLUB

Looking for New York City's newest tennis and squash club? Make sure to look up! The opulent, 80,000 square foot CityView Racquet Club was built atop the iconic 1930s Swingline Stapler factory. The multilevel club's first floor begins fifty feet above ground level.

This section of Long Island City was, at one time, almost exclusively industrial, but with easy access to and wonderful views of Manhattan, this neighborhood has been "discovered." A massive Con-Edison power plant, movie studios, corporate headquarters, full-service high rise apartment buildings and now a luxury racquet club all call Long Island City home. City View offers anyone willing to purchase a day pass this unique opportunity to taste country club life in the midst of urban renewal.

While the entire ultra-modern club was built on a rooftop, the four squash and seven tennis courts, as well as the luxury spa and fitness facilities, are indoors. But CityView Racquet Club takes advantage of its height and unobstructed views with an inviting and expansive rooftop patio. Even though it is called a "club," nonmembers are welcome to enjoy all the premium amenities this facility has to offer, including its rooftop bar and terrace. Pining for a post-tennis match margarita with a view? Look up in Long Island City and your wishes will be granted.

City Ice Pavilion

Location: Long Island City, Queens

Address: 47-32 32nd Place, Long Island City, Queens, NY 11101

Phone: 718.706.6667

www.cityicepavilion.com

Subway:

Subway Stop: 33rd St-Rawson

Calendar: Year-round

Hours: Updated weekly on website

$

Photos courtesy of City Ice Pavilion

99. CITY ICE PAVILION

When the New York City summer heat and humidity become unbearable, grab your parka and escape to a chilly winter wonderland. The one-of-a-kind rooftop ice rink, City Ice Pavilion is the place to cool off, have some old-fashioned fun and even get a little exercise during summer, or anytime of year.

Opened in 2008 by a hockey-loving dad who wanted a place for his kids to skate, this bubble-enclosed National Hockey League regulation-size rink dwarfs many of the outdoor winter skating options in Manhattan. At 85 by 200 feet, there is plenty of room for beginners and old pros to glide around, especially during the more sparsely attended midweek public sessions. For spectators, free bleachers are provided, but with the affordable ice time and skate rental rates, everyone should try a spin on the ice. It is kept very cold under the bubble, so the best way to stay cozy is to keep moving on those skates. For those who choose to watch from the bleachers, make sure to bring a hat, scarf and gloves, even in summer.

While it is only a quick subway ride, plus a short walk, from Manhattan to City Ice Pavilion, the facility is built on a three-story commercial site surrounded by warehouse-type buildings. It is an area with a notable lack of pedestrians and dining choices, so be sure to have your walking directions and your brown-bag lunch in hand once you exit the subway station.

100. ROOFTOP FILMS

Hit the roof explorers' jackpot with the Rooftop Films' Summer Series. Each year between May and August, visit as many as seven otherwise inaccessible New York City rooftops for this outdoor, avant garde cinema festival. Scores of movies by emerging and established filmmakers are shown to tens of thousands of people in outdoor venues stretching from the Bronx to the Rockaways, but be sure to look for the following rooftop venues (subject to change so check the website):

- The Bronx Terminal Market near Yankee Stadium

- Pier 15, the Manhattan double-decker pier jutting out 500 feet into the East River (Roof #50, pp. 112-113)

- Rooftop Films headquarters at The Old American Can Factory in Gowanus, Brooklyn

- The rooftop of Residences at the W New York-Downtown

- The Lower East Side rooftop of The New Design High School

- Two expansive rooftops at Industry City in Brooklyn

- The Trilock Fusion Center for the Arts, also in Brooklyn

This nonprofit arts organization began quite by accident in 1997 when a recent college graduate set up an inexpensive sound system and hoisted a white sheet for use as a screen. He invited friends to the roof of the East Village tenement building where he lived and showed short films well into the night. Nearly two decades later, there are seven full-time employees and scores of dedicated interns and volunteers expanding this rooftop grassroots arts organization.

Rooftop Films

Location: Bronx, Brooklyn and Lower Manhattan

Address: 232 3rd St. Suite E-103, Brooklyn, NY 11215

Phone: 718.417.7362

www.rooftopfilms.com

Best way to get there: Bicycle

Calendar: May-Aug

Hours: At dusk

Reservations: Recommended

$

Photo by Ari Burling

Openhousenewyork Weekend (OHNY)

www.ohny.org

Calendar: One weekend in October

Reservations: Yes

$

Photo by Heather Shimmin

101. OPENHOUSENEWYORK WEEKEND (OHNY)

Unlike the 100 accessible New York City rooftops you've been guided to so far, this final listing offers you something slightly different: directions to some of New York's inaccessible rooftops.

Beginning in 2003, New York City imported London's great annual architectural weekend celebration. Called "Open House New York (OHNY)," and occurring for just one jam-packed weekend each October, this city-wide event allows the general public inside, or, in the case of roof explorers, on top of, buildings with rare access.

Although the sites change annually, rooftops have been included every year. Past OHNY weekends have included tours of the near impossible-to-visit formal gardens on top of Rockefeller Center; the many roof elevations, including a rooftop orchard, of the Via Verde

housing complex; the green roof at Pratt Institute; a preview of the then-undeveloped final section of the High Line; as well as access into architecturally significant private homes with green roofs or rooftop gardens.

In order to control the crowds for the most popular destinations, OHNY implemented a reservation policy for many of its sites. The booklet listing that year's hundreds of OHNY sites is available only days before the Weekend event. Therefore, getting the maximum roof exploring out of this brief opportunity requires a careful strategy:

1. Get the OHNY booklet as soon as it is made available (this date will be posted online by mid-September), usually just a few days before the OHNY Weekend.

2. Scour the booklet for rooftop venues, as there is no separate rooftop section in the guide. Read quickly though, as reservations can fill up fast.

3. List the times when the rooftops are open (some are only open one of the two weekend days, or at specific times), and make your plans. Be sure to leave enough travel time from one rooftop destination to the next.

4. Go to the website (ohny.org), credit card in hand, and make the inexpensive reservations. You will get an email confirmation.

5. During OHNY Weekend, rain or shine, go roof exploring!

SUGGESTED ITINERARIES

The following are some suggestions on combining rooftop visits in a single day or evening. With such a variety of rooftops available, please use these suggestions as a starting point to create routes that match your individual interests.

1. Family-friendly Stroll and Lunch

Ride the Pier 62 Carousel
(#61, pp. 136-137) (open between May-Oct)

Enter The High Line via the 20th Street and 10th Avenue staircase. Walk south to the exit at Gansevoort Street (#52, pp. 116-117)

Enjoy a pint and lunch at The Brass Monkey
(#33, pp. 78-79)

2. Citi Bike Downtown Manhattan Roof Tour

Start at Pier 15 (#50, pp. 112-113)

See the Elevated Acre (#49, pp. 110-111)

Walk through the Irish Hunger Memorial
(#48, pp. 108-109)

Enjoy a sunset drink at The Loopy Doopy Bar
(#1, pp. 12-13) (open May-Sept)

3. Upscale Bar Hopping for Trendsetters

Enjoy a crepe and a drink at Le Bain at the Standard Hotel (#5, pp. 20-21)

Catch the sunset from STK Roof
(#31, pp. 74-75) (open only May-Oct)

Try a cocktail at PH-D at the Dream Downtown
(#6, pp. 22-23)

4. Stylish Rooftop Dinner and Drinks

Relax with a pre-dinner drink at Bookmarks at the Library Hotel (#13, pp. 36-37)

Dine at The Bryant Park Grill (#39, pp. 90-91)
(open May-September)

Take a long walk or a cab ride for a nightcap at the Press Lounge at Ink 48 Hotel (#17, pp. 44-45)

5. Explore Williamsburg, Brooklyn

Brunch at Berry Park (#44, pp. 98-99)

Enjoy the view at Bushwick Inlet Park
(#69, pp. 150-151)

Finish with drinks at Upper Elm at the King & Grove Hotel (#26, pp. 62-63) or The Ides Bar at the Wythe Hotel (#24, pp. 58-59)

6. Feed your Body and Soul in Morningside Heights

Experience The Vertical Tour at The Cathedral Church of St. John the Divine (#67, pp. 146-147) (Wednesdays and Saturdays only)

Stop in for a casual meal at The Heights Bar & Grill (#42, pp. 95)

7. Rooftops for Active People

Fly through the air at a Trapeze School New York class (#88, pp. 192-193) (May-Oct only)

Cool off at City Ice Pavilion (#99, pp. 214-215)

Warm up at Russian &Turkish Baths (#87, pp. 190-191) or try a yoga class at YoYoga! (#94, pp. 204-205)

8. Theater Lovers Rooftops

Explore the Robert Moses Plaza rooftop at Fordham University (#53, pp. 118-119)

Relax on the Laurie M. Tisch Illumination Lawn at Lincoln Center (#54, pp. 120-121)

Catch a show at The Claire Tow Theater (#64, pp. 140-141)

Have dinner and drinks at Gallow Green (#36, pp. 84-85) (open May-September)

9. Science Lovers Rooftops

Tour the 5 Boro Roof Garden on Randall's Island (#81, pp. 176-177) (by appointment only)

Stargaze at The Rutherford Observatory (#97, pp. 210-211) (every other Friday night during the academic year)

10. Big Spenders

Shop along Fifth Avenue with a stop at Trump Towers Privately Owned Public Spaces (#55, pp. 122-123)

Sip cocktails with a view at Salon de Ning (#21, pp. 52-53)

Spend the night at The Outdoor Bedroom at AKA (#19, pp. 48-49)

11. History Buffs Rooftop Adventures

Pay tribute at The National September 11 Memorial (#57, pp. 128-129) (free, but best to reserve in advance)

See the view from Garden of Stones at the Museum of Jewish Heritage (#58, pp. 130-131)

Ride the Staten Island Ferry then hop on a bus to Fort Tompkins and Battery Weed (#75, pp. 162-163)

INDEX:

230 Fifth, 82

5 Boro Green Roof Garden, 176

9/11 Memorial, 129

Above Rooftop (Hilton Garden Inn Staten Island), 67

AKA Central Park Hotel, 48

Alexandria Center (Riverpark), 115

Aloft Hotel (Brooklyn Terrace), 60

Annual Kite Flight at the Port Authority Bus Terminal, 203

Arsenal at Central Park, 142

Asphalt Green Rooftop Terrace, 208

Atlantic Terminal Subway Entrance at Barclays Center, 152

Ava Lounge (Dream Hotel), 46

Bar d'Eau (Trump SoHo New York), 15

Barclays Center, 60

Batali/Bastianich, 80

Battery Weed, 127, 163

Beer Authority, 89

Bentley Hotel (Prime), 57

Berry Park Beer Garden, 99

Bike Rentals, 9

Bocce Court, 15

Bohemian National Hall Rooftop Terrace, 206

Bookmarks (Library Hotel), 37

Bowery Mission, 134

Brass Monkey, 69, 79

Broadway Stages, 178

Bronx County Courthouse, 158

Bronx Terminal Market, 217

Brooklyn Botanic Garden Visitor Center, 127, 148

Brooklyn Bridge Park, 100, 154

Brooklyn Grange Farm, 165, 169

Brooklyn Grange Farm at The Brooklyn Navy Yard, 180

Brooklyn Grange Flagship Farm in Long Island City, Queens, 186

Brooklyn Terrace (Aloft Hotel), 60

Bryant Park Grill, 91

Bushwick Inlet Park Facilities Building, 151

Carousel, 124, 136

Central Park, 48, 142, 144

Chelsea Market Passage, 76

Chicken Coop, 179

Chrysler Building, 43, 65

Citi Bike, 9

City Ice Pavilion, 214

CityView Racquet Club, 212

Claire Tow Theater 2, 120, 141

Columbia Astronomy Public Outreach 95, 189, 210

Conrad Hotel (Loopy Doopy), 13

Courtyard by Marriot (Monarch Rooftop), 30

Creperie, 21

Crosby Hotel (Rooftop Kitchen Garden), 166

Czech Center, 189, 206

Delancey, 72

Dream Downtown (PH-D Rooftop Lounge), 22

Dream Hotel (Ava Lounge), 46

Eagle Bar NYC, 87

Eagle Street Rooftop Farm, 178

East River Esplanade, 110, 112

Eataly (La Birreria), 80

Elevated Acre, 110, 122

Elinor Bunin Munroe Film Center, 120

Empire Hotel (Rooftop and Pool Deck), 54

Empire State Building 27, 29, 33, 39, 82, 172, 199

Fairfield Inn and Suites (Sky Room), 38

Farm Dinners, 170, 181

Farm Tours, 170

Farm-In-The-Sky (FITS), 184

Fashion Center Business Improvement District, 203

Fire pits/Fireplaces, 37,67

Fireboat House, 132

Flanner, Ben, 178, 186

Flatiron Building, 195

Fordham University (Robert Moses Plaza), 118

Fort Schuyler (Bronx), 160

Fort Tompkins, 127, 163

Gallow Green (McKittrick Hotel), 69, 85

Gansevoort Park Rooftop, 29

Garden of Stones (Museum of Jewish Heritage), 130

GE Building, 200

German Beer Garden, 99

Gilberto, Bebel, 27

Goldsworthy, Andy, 130, 144

Gotham Greens, 165

Gowanus Canal, 182

Gramercy Terrace (Gramercy Park Hotel), 24, 25

Green Roof Systems, 176

Hammock, 50

Happy Hour, 39, 40, 54, 60, 72, 97

Heights Bar & Grill, 95

Henry's Rooftop Bar (Roger Smith Hotel), 43

High Line, 27, 75, 76, 107, 116, 219

High Line Food Court, 76

Hilton Garden Inn Staten Island (Above Rooftop), 67

Hot Tub, 27

Hotel Americano (La Piscine), 27

Hotel Chantelle, 70

Hudson Hotel (Sky Terrace), 50

Hydroponics, 182

Ides (Wythe Hotel), 11, 58, 151

Ink 48 Hotel (Press Lounge), 44

Iris and B. Gerald Cantor Roof Garden at Metropolitan Museum of Art, 48, 144

Irish Hunger Memorial, 108

James Hotel (Jimmy), 11, 16

Jazz, 54

Jazz Brunch, 70

Jimmy (James Hotel), 11, 16

King & Grove Williamsburg (Upper Elm), 63

Kosher, 57

La Birreria (Eataly), 80

La Piscine (Hotel Americano), 10, 26, 27

Larry Flynt's Hustler Club New York (Roof Deck and Cigar Lounge), 93

Laurie M. Tisch Illumination Lawn, 120

Le Bain (Standard High Line), 6, 20, 21

Library Hotel (Bookmarks), 37

Lincoln Center (Claire Tow Theater), 141

Loopy Doopy (Conrad Hotel), 12, 13

Lower East Side (LES) Ecology Center, 132

Lower East Side Girls Club, 138

Madison Square Park (Shake Shack), 139

Malibu Rooftop Deck

(Yankee Stadium), 102

Maritime Industry Museum, 161

Massage, 54

Metropolitan Museum of Art (Iris and B. Gerald Cantor Roof Garden), 144

Midtown Tennis Club, 196

MoMA, 48, 53

Monarch Rooftop (Courtyard by Marriot), 30

Mondrian SoHo (Soaked), 19

Municipal Asphalt Plant, 208

Museum of Jewish Heritage (Garden of Stones), 130

National Record of Historic Places, 158, 162

National September 11 Memorial, 129

New Design High School, 217

New York City Marathon, 162

New York Philharmonic, 141

New York Public Library, 37, 91

New York Public Library

for the Performing Arts, 141

Novak, Annie, 178

Observation Deck, Empire State Building, 199

Old American Can Factory, 217

Openhousenewyork Weekend (OHNY), 218

Peninsula Hotel (Salon de Ning), 11, 53

PH-D Rooftop Lounge (Dream Hotel), 22

Pickens, Zach, 170

Pier 15 at the East River Esplanade, 112, 217

Pier 5 Ample Hills Creamery at Brooklyn Bridge Park, 154

Pier 62 Carousel at Hudson River Park, 136

Pine Bar & Grill, 105

Pod 39 Hotel, 34

Pool, 16, 29, 54, 107, 124

Port Authority Bus Terminal, 38, 89, 203

Press Lounge (Ink 48 Hotel), 44

Prime (Bentley Hotel), 57

Privately Owned Public Spaces (POPS), 110, 122

Pupin Hall Rooftop at Columbia University, 210, 189

Queens Botanical Garden Visitor & Administration Building, 156

Queensboro Bridge, 57, 65, 204

Randall's Island, 176, 177

RCA Building, 200

Red Shirt Rooftop Reading Series, 195

Refinery Rooftop at The Refinery Hotel, 33

River to River Festival, 110

Riverbank State Park, 123

Riverbank State Park Community Garden, 174

Riverpark (restaurant and public space) (Alexandria Center), 115

Riverpark Farm at Alexandria Center, 170

Robert Moses Plaza (Fordham University), 118

Rock Shop, 69, 96

Rockefeller Center, 200

Roger Smith Hotel (Henry's Rooftop Bar), 43

Rollins, Artie, 177

Roof Deck and Cigar Lounge (Larry Flynt's Hustler Club New York), 93

Rooftop and Pool Deck (Empire Hotel), 54

Rooftop at Pod 39 Hotel, 34

Rooftop Brewery, 80

Rooftop Films, 189, 217

Rooftop Kitchen Garden (The Crosby Hotel), 166

Rooftop Reggae, 63

Rosemary's, 169

Russian and Turkish Baths, 191

Rutherford Observatory, 210

Salon de Ning (Peninsula Hotel), 11, 53

Semi-intensive green roof, 148

Shake Shack (Madison Square Park), 139

Skating rink, 124, 214

Sky Room (Fairfield Inn and Suites), 38

Sky Room at the New Museum, 134

Sky Terrace (Hudson Hotel), 50

Sleep No More, 85

Smith, Ken, 53, 110

Soaked (Mondrian SoHo), 18, 19

Standard High Line (Le Bain), 21

Statue of Liberty, 13, 100, 108, 130

STK Rooftop NYC, 75

Stuyvesant, Peter, 134

Suggested Itineraries, 220

Swingline Stapler Factory, 212

Terrace at YOTEL New York, 40

Terrace, Midtown 1015 at Sutton Place, 94

Theater District, 40, 46

Throgs Neck Bridge, 160

Times Square, 39

Top of the Rock®, 200

Trapeze School New York, 189, 192

Triborough Bridge, 176, 177

Trilock Fusion Center, 217

Trump SoHo (Bar d'Eau), 15

Trump Tower, 122

Upper Elm (King & Grove Williamsburg), 63, 151

Verrazano Narrows Bridge, 127

Vertical Tour (Cathedral Church of St. John the Divine), 146

Via Verde, 218

Waldorf Astoria Rooftop Garden, 172

Wallabout Bay, 180

War of 1812, 160

Washington, George, 132, 162

Whiteread, Rachel (Water Tower), 53

Whitney Museum, 75

Whole Foods Market® Rooftop Farm and The Roof, 165, 182

Wythe Hotel (Ides), 11, 58

Yankee Stadium (Malibu Rooftop Deck), 102, 159

YOTEL New York (Terrace at YOTEL New York), 40

YoYoga!, 204

Z Roof (Z Hotel New York), 65

ABOUT THE AUTHOR

Leslie Adatto, Author and Roof Explorer

Gary Schacker

Leslie Adatto has been seeking out New York City rooftops since relocating to Manhattan in 2010. She blogs about New York City rooftops (lookingupwithleslie.com) and organizes two active Meetup groups, The New York Roof Deck and Roof Gardening Meetup Group and Rooftop Drinkers NYC. Leslie earned a BA in English from UCLA, is a former high school teacher and runs a bicoastal business. Leslie lives, bikes and cooks in the West Village.

PHOTO CREDITS

Heather Shimmin, Photographer

Heather Shimmin received a BFA in Photography from Utah Valley University and an MA in Historical and Sustainable Architecture from NYU London. Her capstone thesis was on Green Roofs in London. Heather believes rooftops are panaceas for cities, mitigating the effects of the Urban Heat Island Effect, storm water runoff, overpopulation, and lack of public space. *heathershimmin.com*

Ari Burling, Photographer

Ari Burling is a New York City-based commercial artist specializing in architectural photography and images of the built environment. He earned his BFA in Photography from Parsons School of Design in 1995 and has since been working professionally throughout the United States. His images have appeared in Metropolis, Contract, Architectural Record, and Architect's Journal magazines. *ariburling.com*

DESIGN CREDITS

Arlene Bender, Bob Aiese, Designers

Arlene and Bob have an extensive list of clients that span their combined 80 years of creative design experience including fashion, medical, home, photography to video, illustration, catalog, magazine, print, web and various mulitimedia.

Acknowledgements:

When I began my fascination with urban rooftops, I was a brand-new New York City transplant who knew three people in my freshly adopted home town. A few years later, I have had the privilege of getting to know, and of receiving enormous generosity from, scores of New Yorkers who have shared my passion to create this first-of-its-kind guidebook. My heartfelt thanks go out to all of you. So many pitched in, you'd think we were building a barn rather than making a book.

I feel compelled to mention a few of you who went above and beyond, and always nodded yes when I'd call and ask, yet again, for another favor.

Thank you so much to Bob Aiese and Arlene Bender, an amazing couple who have designed and typeset this gorgeous little gem. You have been beyond patient and generous to a fault with your novice self-publisher.

Ari Burling and Heather Shimmin: you took time from your hectic lives to photograph roofs with me in sometimes freezing, occasionally wet and often unbearably hot weather. I also have to mention Rhea Alexander, who cheerfully grabbed her equipment, hopped on her bike along side me and filled in as my photographer when I was in a pinch.

Laura Brown volunteered her extraordinary editorial skills and unflinching moral support on countless occasions, and Bridget Gramling offered invaluable proofreading assistance. Michelle Brick, my intern-turned-friend: your unrelenting encouragement groomed me into New York City's roof explorer. Karen Seiger: your niche travel guide and optimism inspired me to make this book happen, and Caroline Goff: your kindness and kinesiology balances kept me on track. Thanks so much to all of these exceptional women.

Finally, I must mention George Ludwig. You believed in this book even when I would wake up with stomach-churning doubts. Thank you for biking the five boroughs with me and keeping me laughing.